A Caddie Remembers

Golf in the 1930s

by

Joseph H. Cowan

authorHOUSE™

1663 Liberty Drive, Suite 200
Bloomington, Indiana 47403
(800) 839-8640
www.AuthorHouse.com

© 2004 Joseph H. Cowan
All Rights Reserved.

No part of this book may be reproduced, stored in a retrieval system, or transmitted by any means without the written permission of the author.

First published by AuthorHouse 12/14/04

ISBN: 1-4184-9357-0 (sc)

Library of Congress Control Number: 2004096848

Printed in the United States of America
Bloomington, Indiana

This book is printed on acid-free paper.

FRONT COVER

1930s golf clubs provided by Mr. Stanley Hall and photo by Mrs. Sandra Hall Correnti, both of Marin County, California.

Clubs l. to r: Bobby Jones 7-iron by Spalding ca. 1934, Hillerich and Bradsby Fairway Iron, ca 1926 (175-200 yards), Biltmore Mashie, Ky Lafoon Brassie (No.2) by Spalding ca. 1934, Hillerich and Bradsby Pitching Mashie, ca 1926 (85-120 yards) and Bobby Jones 4-iron by Spalding ca 1934.

ACKNOWLEDGMENTS

Laurel Olson Cook Healdsburg, California (laurelcook@comcast. net) What began as an author-editor situation evolved into author-mentor. In addition to running a home-based editorial business she is an established writer and I shall always be grateful for her invaluable help that went from editing to organizing, formatting and providing guidance into the mysteries of Microsoft Word.

ANN GERDOM Western Golf Association/Evans Scholars Foundation Ms. Gerdom walked the extra mile in providing information about the WGA/ESF. Without her help I would not have known about the lasting legacy of Chick Evans who established a foundation that has provided college educations to some 8,000 qualifying caddies. Nor would I have known that he (Evans) won both the 1916 U. S. Open and U. S. Amateur using but seven hickory shaft clubs.

J. PETER MARTIN Lake Placid, New York: Head Golf Professional at the Whiteface Club, chronicler of golf in the Adirondacks, and biographer who graciously gave permission to use part of his *Craig Wood, Blonde Bomber and Son of Lake Placid* to supplement my personal knowledge. I have given full attribution where I took advantage of his offer.

PATTI MORAN United States Golf Association virtually opened the USGA library to me. When I asked for a specific item of information it came by return mail. She was the source of information about instances that I could not possibly have witnessed. But for her this book would be smaller and less accurate.

DR. FRANK QUINN, Metropolitan Golf Association: During the period covered by this book the Metropolitan Open was a major tournament and a list of its winners was essential to a balanced account. When I asked him his response was thorough and immediate.

TABLE OF CONTENTS

ACKNOWLEDGMENTS v

PREFACE ix

INTRODUCTION xi

HARD TIMES 1

THE STATE OF THE GAME 5

WHAT THINGS COST 8

CADDIE DAYS 10

OTHER CADDIES 15

ABOUT THE PLAYERS 19

WHEN THEY PLAYED 25

HOW THEY ARRIVED: THE DEL MONTE SPECIAL 26

STORIES THE PARKING LOTS TOLD 28

HOW PLAYERS DRESSED 30

WHAT THEY DRANK 33

ABOUT THE PROS 35

THE CELEBRITIES, TITANS, AND STARS 39

THE EQUIPMENT 65

GOLF BAGS 66

GOLF CLUBS 68

THE GOLF COURSES 80

DRIVING RANGES 83

TEE BOXES 85

TEES	86
WALKERS ONLY.	87
SLOW PLAY	89
THE STYMIE RULE	92
THE UNIFYING ODOR	94
RAIN AND LIGHTNING.	96
TOURNAMENTS	99
WHAT'S IN A NAME?	100
IMPORTANT DEVELOPMENTS POST 1930	109
BUSINESS GOLF	113
SUGGESTED READING	117

PREFACE

In late 2000, I was in the hospital. A senior attendant, a true golf enthusiast, liked to bring other staff members to my bedside to introduce them to me as a veteran of World War II and a man who had vivid memories of golf in the 1930s. It is their abiding interest and questions that led me to start this book—not about my role in the war, which was minor, but about my life in golf. Thousands of others could have written about golf in its early decades, but most are no longer living and those who are probably didn't have my good fortune to be hospitalized among such an inquisitive and encouraging bedside audience.

What I write about here will be new to my living friends, who first knew me as a commissioned officer in the World War II Army, not a Depression kid with a love of golf, and much of it also be new to my wife, Marjorie, and children, daughter Michele and sons Joseph and James to whom I dedicate this book.

INTRODUCTION

Golf came to the United States beginning about 1885, though President Ulysses S. Grant had been exposed to it some years earlier while touring the British Isles. Legend has it that he was taken to a golf course, given a club and a golf ball and invited to take a whack. He whiffed the ball a few times and said, "It's a grand game; but I don't see the use of the ball".

The United States Golf Association (USGA) was founded in late 1894. It was "first in time," a legal term for being there before anyone else, and it marked the formal organization of golf in the United States. The USGA was responsible for writing the rules, conducting national championships and creating a national system of handicapping.

In 1920 it founded its Green Section to advise member clubs on matters of maintenance and management of golf courses and to fund research on improving strains of turf grass that require less watering and are more tolerant of stress.

At first the USGA took some criticism because golfers in other parts of the country thought it snooty and felt that its Northeast location placed it out of touch. Other regional golf associations even had their own rules. Time eroded this feeling and when I came to golf in 1930 the USGA had become the unquestioned arbiter of golf in the United States and Mexico.

The Metropolitan Golf Association was founded in the spring of 1897 to serve golf clubs within 55 miles of New York City. The territory has since expanded and the original 23 member clubs now number 500 and serve 120,000 golfers. The association has always conducted an extensive tournament program; for example, Maureen Orcutt's first victory was the Metropolitan Junior Girls Tournament in 1922, and the winner list of the Metropolitan Open during the 1930s includes the most prominent tour players.

The Western Golf Association was founded in 1899 by eleven Chicago-area golf clubs. It now has more than 500 member clubs and has sponsored the Western Open and the Western Amateur since 1899 and the Western Junior since 1914. Since 1930 it has administered the Chick Evans Caddie Scholarship program that has provided college educations to more than 8,000 former caddies.

HARD TIMES

Between 1930 and 1939 the Depression hung over the United States like a menacing cloud. There is no way to write anything about the 1930s without mentioning it. Remember, there were no federal unemployment insurance programs and no Social Security. Unemployment stood at 25%. Personal bankruptcies were filed only by the truly desperate because to do so was considered most disgraceful.

Very soon after Franklin D. Roosevelt became president of the United States in 1933 the Works Progress Administration (WPA as it came to be known) was established to put people to work. It built public works and created jobs for musicians, writers, historians, laborers, actors and others who had been struggling. Much of what it accomplished was of lasting value (for example, wilderness trails and clubhouses for municipal golf courses) but there were some god-awful boondoggles. One story circulating at the time was about a property owner who called the WPA and asked that his lawn be mowed. A truck showed up at his house and disgorged two lawnmowers, eight laborers, a foreman and a two-seat portable toilet. When the owner asked the foreman what was going on he was told, "Two a comin', two a goin', two a sittin', two a mowin.'"

Thousands of homes were foreclosed when the owners could not make their loan payments. But often lenders got a nasty surprise when they found that the owner who had not been able to make loan payments also had not been able to pay real estate taxes and insurance premiums. So the lenders had to pay back taxes and insurance premiums in order to protect their investments. That is why the newly created Federal Housing Administration (FHA) required that monthly payments include one-twelfth of the estimated tax and insurance costs to be held by the lenders who would pay taxes and insurance premiums as they fell due.

Many country clubs suffered fatal financial problems and were foreclosed. Some wound up in the hands of individuals who hoped to operate them profitably. In other cases the obligations were so massive the club properties were abandoned. The Oak Knoll Country Club in Oakland went to foreclosure in 1933 or so and was bought by an individual, who operated it with reasonable success until the outbreak of World War II when the U. S. Navy took it over, demolished the golf course and built a hospital. Only the clubhouse was left standing for use by patients and staff. Castlewood Country Club, situated in Pleasanton, California on the estate of the late Phoebe Apperson Hearst, mother of William Randolph Hearst, had failed about 1932, was bought by an investor who ran it until in the 1950s the area was economically revitalized by the technology boom and it (Castlewood) was reconstituted as a country club.

On the other hand, there was a club (whose name I never learned) situated on Crow Canyon Road between Castro Valley and Danville, California that just shriveled away. By 1939 it had reverted to weeds, except for an abandoned and vandalized clubhouse.

Many people who should have known better thought that the party would never end and spearheaded the establishment of new country clubs and the remodeling of existing clubs. Some spectacular failures caused cynics to grin and observe that the creation of or major remodeling of country clubs foretold difficult times.

Economic reverses led many members to resign from their clubs. At one club in Indianapolis resigned members held a meeting to select the public course they would play and thus retain the companionship they had known before they had to cut back. We caddies thought it a coup that they chose our course, Willowbrook, expecting an increase in business that never materialized.

A man I met after I joined the Olympic Club in 1968, was graduated from St, Mary's College in 1933, was very glad to get a gardening job at the San Francisco Golf Club. He later became a member of the Olympic Club and lived in a house bordering the 16th hole of its Ocean Course. When age caused him to give up golf he would hang over the fence and talk with golf companions he had known all his life. He seldom failed to relate how lucky he had been to have any job at all during those troubled times.

Joseph H. Cowan

Another pro arranged with his physician to give golf lessons to the physician's son in exchange for the family's medical treatment.

Eddie: I met him in 1935 when he came from heaven knows where to the Willowbrook public golf course in Indianapolis where he was clubhouse steward, making superb sandwiches, cleaning shoes and keeping the locker room shipshape. I'll never forget the wonderful hamburger and pork tenderloin sandwiches he sold to caddies for 10 cents and to golfers for 25 cents. Today when I make a sandwich I try to season it the way Eddie did, using salt, pepper and Worcestershire Sauce but I never get the proportions right.

A father figure to Willowbrook caddies; he was an example of the pervasive loss of status and income that accompanied the Depression. As far as I know, he did not receive a salary; his only income derived from the profit he made selling sandwiches and tips from shining shoes. He taught me a lot, especially not to complain. Although he had experienced racial discrimination all his life, he exuded cheer in everything he did. He never mentioned where he lived or if he had a family. All I knew about his past was that he had been either a sleeping car porter or a parlor car attendant on the New York Central Railroad until he was furloughed, railroad talk for laid off.

Good old Willowbrook has long been plowed under and urbanized and Eddie is surely dead by now. I don't have much time left myself but I take comfort in knowing that, when I get to the Pearly Gates, Eddie will be waiting. Only then will I learn his surname.

THE STATE OF THE GAME

Before TV, golf had little mass appeal. Indeed, about 1934 *The American Golfer*, the then bible of golf, carried an article saying that golf would never be a spectator sport. Despite the explosion of interest in golf in the 1920s, many still thought that it was played only by the snooty; they held it in low esteem and snickered at those who played what some called Cow Pasture Pool. If you were playing a hole that was bordered by a road, there was a good chance of being taunted by someone in a passing car yelling "Fore." If the vehicle were a Model T Ford touring car with the top either down or removed entirely, and carrying young people, taunting was a certainty.

In those years when you went to a movie, part of the standard fare was a newsreel showing current events that would frequently include snippets of golf tournaments. These and Exhibition Matches, played with almost the regularity of a touring theatrical company, brought golf to the public.

Joseph H. Cowan

Exhibition Matches would feature a prominent pro or pros engaged to play with locals under arrangements designed to draw a paying gallery.

"Prominent" was a relative term. It could be a big city pro with regional success recruited by a small town that had a larger-than-normal group of golf fans. Or the prominence could be tied to the venue; one that would be satisfied with nothing less than nationally known players. If you wanted to observe good golf without actually being at the scene of the tournament, you either attended an Exhibition Match or saw tournament play in a newsreel.

If you want to *see* how the game was played in the early 1930s, go to your local video store and rent *Bagger Vance*. It is a faultless reconstruction of the then popular "Exhibition Match" that shows how they dressed and the equipment they used. Just as accurately it shows the clothes worn those by the gallery. Yes, once upon a time people did dress to attend a golf match. I smiled knowingly at a scene in the film where darkness was descending and the players had just finished the 17th hole. Automobiles were circled around the 18th green, headlights blazing, to provide illumination. Unlikely? No. I saw this in 1935 at a weekly Pro-Am held in Fortville, Indiana.

The first electronic breakthrough came in the late twenties when NBC began to cover golf events with a two-person radio team, one doing the talking and the other carrying the equipment, (just as you see in the Korean War memorial depicting an infantry platoon on patrol.) Communications equipment did not become carry-in-your-pocket small until some years later when the transistor replaced the vacuum tube

There were many ladies tournaments in the years between 1895 and World War II, all of which were for amateurs, so many in fact that a tournament took place nearly every week of the year, conducted by state and local golf associations and by resort owners seeking press exposure. It wasn't until the late 40s that the Ladies Professional Golf Association was founded.

WHAT THINGS COST

What things cost in those years gives you some perspective: Caddie fees were one dollar per bag for 18 holes. 25 cents per hour for shagging balls and 25 cents for delivering a message to a player on the course. Top-of-the-line golf balls cost 75 cents. Green fees at municipal courses were no more than one dollar per round. A can of Shinola shoe polish cost 10 cents.

Leading brands of golf shoes were Florsheim, Keith Highlanders, Spalding and McAfee (English). All cost about $20. Regal Shoes at about $10 were knockoffs and advertised as such. Thom McAn (sic) golf shoes cost $3.33 and were big sellers, especially among caddies.

Soft drinks and candy bars cost five cents. When Three Musketeers first came to market the name really meant something because buyers got three separate pieces. Now they consist of but one piece but the name remains the same.

Standard brands of cigarettes were 20 cents per pack, but at the depth of the Depression you could buy Wings for 10 cents per pack. Cigars labeled "Factory Throwouts" were two for five cents.

Golf club prices ranged downward from ten dollars for irons and fifteen dollars for woods. I learned of the most expensive woods only by reading the MacGregor catalog. At twenty-five dollars each they were too expensive to be carried in most pro shops.

Individual lessons cost five dollars and group lessons cost five dollars per person for six half-hour lessons.

It is against this historical backdrop that my life as a caddie unfolded.

CADDIE DAYS

My love affair with golf began in 1930 when I became a caddie. It was the year Bobby Jones won the Grand Slam, halfway through Herbert Hoover's presidency; and three years before Hitler came to power. Only two years earlier Ford had phased out its Model T three-pedal planetary transmission and introduced its first stick shift. Automatic transmissions and TV sets would not be widely available on the market for about twenty years.

When I was in the fifth grade at St. Joan of Arc School in Indianapolis Someone brought golf balls to school and we soon discovered that they were great toys. Dropped to the sidewalk or thrown against a wall they responded with resounding bounces. Remove the covers and see an apparently endless string of rubber that invited every boy of a certain age to unravel and, at the center, find a core shaped like the yolk of a hard-boiled egg. Naturally we had to cut the core open to see the mysterious white substance.

Exploring the mystery of the golf ball led to discussions about what caddies earned. My blue-collar family, dysfunctional in many ways, always worked hard, and their example inspired me. So I went to the Meridian Hills Country Club in northern Indianapolis and persuaded the Caddie Master to take me on. I was eleven years old

Sunday was a busy day and, as you can imagine, the parish clergy took a dim view of young boys missing Sunday Mass to caddy.

One of the perks of being a blue-collar kid attending a parochial school and being a caddie at a country club was the opportunity to see how the other half lived. At St. Joan of Arc School and at the country club I learned some social graces that otherwise would have eluded me.

About 1932 a new public course, Willowbrook, opened. It was within walking distance of my home and, as walking and hitchhiking were the only ways we kids got from place to place, I went to work there, though I do not recall just what I did to be accepted. I don't think that the owner thought of it as a hire. He had other things on his mind, such as what would happen to his leisure-time investment during the dreadful economic pinch.

If I picked up a little polish at the country club, it was at the public course that I learned about life. For example, never wager unless you can pay if you lose all bets; never ask a question if the answer might be, "none of your business," never complain if you play poorly; and do not assume that a couple are married just because they live together.

Joseph H. Cowan

At Meridian Hills Country Club I had been a caddie, period. But things were different at the new public course. Pro shop, business office and caddie area were so configured that ordinary privacy was out of the question. So, except for what went on in the living quarters of the owner-manager, I learned something about almost everything there is to know about operating a golf course.

Being a caddie consists mostly of waiting and so I had plenty of time to overhear conversations and to read. Besides the rulebooks and supplier catalogs I read a lot of golf-related publications, especially *The American Golfer.*

The fact that I caddied in three major events, the 1935 Indianapolis Open, the USGA's 1935 Amateur Public Links Championship and the 1937 Oakland Open says nothing about my skill level. I just went to the Caddie Master at each course and asked for work. As each of these events occurred in my then hometown, I was able to make do with public transit.

I regret that, in spite of all my exposure to golf, I never played very well. My only win was at the 1934 Indiana State Junior Tournament when I received six-pack of Coca Cola for getting an eagle 2 on the second hole of the Anderson Country Club. The green was so hard that the only way to stay on it was to land the ball on the slope behind and let it roll back down to the green where, hopefully, it would stay. My second shot hit the hill with a grand thump, rolled onto the green and into the hole and there was my eagle 2.

A Caddie Remembers

When I was about 16 and wanted winter income I found a job as a pinsetter at a bowling alley, but gave it up after one try because it scared the wits out of me. Before pin-setting machines were invented only a human could set the pins and return the ball to the bowler. When a bowling ball hit the pins not only did it scatter them but also it made a noise that I would not hear again until I was within earshot of artillery. Although there were shelters inside the pit, much like those that shield matadors in bullrings, the racket and the unpredictable flight of the pins were too much for me.

World War II came and it was goodbye to golf and hello to the Army. During my tour of duty I met, married (and am still married to) First Lieutenant Marjorie Lafaurie, Army Nurse Corps. After leaving the Army, and thanks to the GI Bill of Rights, I attended law school at government expense and was able to buy, with no down payment, one home in Beaverton, Oregon and another in Redwood City, California, the first using my entitlement, the other using my wife's entitlement.

Railroad experience and physical limitations had kept me out of the Army's combat elements and, like so many other soldiers in that position, my country did far more for me than I ever did for my country.

OTHER CADDIES

At the country club, caddies would get together for crap games, usually late on Sunday afternoons. The stakes began low but increased as the losers dropped out and the winners upped their bets. I seldom played because I knew that, given half a chance, the older caddies would take advantage of me.

There were two categories of caddies, the Regulars and the Schoolboys. The Regulars got the first choice of jobs and the Schoolboys got the overflow. Along with my classmate, Carl Taft, later to become a captain in the Oakland Police Department, I became a Schoolboy Semi-Regular (my own term) at Oak Knoll in Oakland. In exchange for sweeping the tree droppings from pro shop and first tee area, we were first out after the Regulars.

The Regulars were those who had finished school, either by graduating or by dropping out, mostly the latter. The Regular I especially remember is "Wingy." Somehow he had lost his left arm just above the elbow, but he managed to play pretty good golf in spite of it. His one-arm back swing took the club to where it should be, and then he loosened his grip, shifted the position of the club, tightened the grip and hit the ball.

Some of the Regulars, I found out, could hardly wait to be paid so they could go downtown, see the strippers at the local burlesque house and then head for the brothel area. Red was a minister's son who, unluckily, had a talent for contracting what then were called venereal diseases. He alternated between being a caddie and being under treatment.

Joe, a deeply religious 17-year-old who decided that he had a calling from God, had arranged to report to the Novitiate on a certain Sunday. The preceding Saturday night he went to a house of ill repute, purportedly to get sex out of his system.

Fats, who was not above manipulating the truth, liked to tell about visiting houses of prostitution that specialized in young girls. When we asked about how things had gone he would laugh and say that he had arrived too early and the girls were still in school.

The Schoolboys were just that: they would show up on Saturdays and Sundays and, as days lengthened, some would come out after school. Some of them had the same preoccupations as the Regulars and dealt with them by reading *Spicy Stories* (actual title) magazines and obscene comic books such as *Popeye the Sailor* and *Tillie the Toiler* (bootlegged cartoon books showing well known images doing very naughty things). The bright side: no parent of a caddie ever had to explain the facts of life.

GM was a tough little 12-year-old from Pennsylvania. All I ever knew about him was that he said had no home and no parents. He simply showed up at Willowbrook one day and became a caddie. "Pittsburgh" came from nowhere, worked for a while and then went out of our lives. He had talked some about riding freight trains hobo-style so we just assumed that he had moved on.

Though they may have been there, I did not see traveling caddies because there was no little money in it. Also I was not privy to the Winners' Circle

Joseph H. Cowan

As they do now, caddies received what their players thought appropriate, nearly always 10% of the prize. The first prize in a major tournament was $1000 but lesser prizes were as little as $50, though I do know of tournaments that paid bottom-rung prizes as little as $12.50.

Some caddies were trustworthy but others were real psychopaths would steal anything not nailed down, and never show a sign of remorse. I soon learned to stay out of their way.

Life was tough for those older caddies who had no family support system. No place to sleep and no money for food if they failed to find work. In the fall some would go to the Plains states to work as harvesters. Mostly they traveled to and from job sites by hopping freight trains and risking three hazards: (1) being injured or killed getting on or off a moving train, (2) being beaten up by the railroad police if they discovered you, and (3) having their shoes stolen any time they drifted off to sleep. Those who returned to caddie duty would talk about the enormous portions of food served by employers who believed that a full stomach makes a productive worker.

Other older caddies who had connections with Caddie Masters in Florida would go down there for the winter.

ABOUT THE PLAYERS

Along the way I caddied for some colorful players who might well have stepped out of the pages of a novel. My first assignment was with a player whose kindness I shall never forget. By the 14th hole I was dragging so badly that he took over, carrying his own clubs for the remainder of the game. He paid me for the full round. Like many to come, I would never see him again.

Count_____never said he was a count; he just acted like one. Though I wondered why a Mediterranean aristocrat would come to land-locked Indianapolis, I never found out. He was well known in mid-Indiana golfing circles and no one seemed to care if his title was genuine or self-bestowed, There were those who said that it had to be genuine because his tailor sewed his pockets shut.

He played respectable golf in a genteel manner. The only time I saw him express aggravation was when he saw another player being abusive to his own caddie. The count said to the caddie, "Tell him you are an American citizen and that he cannot talk to you that way."

AJ and GS were gamblers and bootleggers who decided to take up golf. In addition to their bootlegging talents, it was gossiped that they were highly skilled at dealing "seconds," gambling slang for dealing the card just beneath the card on the top of the deck, without being detected.

They took lesson after lesson though their thick accents made pro-to-student communication difficult. And, at a time when beginners had, say, seven clubs or less and lightweight canvas bags, each had full sets of clubs and caddie-killer golf bags. At first I thought that the pro had oversold them but, as I came to know more about them, I realized that no one in his right mind would try to take advantage of those two.

Mr. and Mrs. BP came to Indianapolis from another city and chose to play at Willowbrook. She had extraordinary good looks and played very well. CR, a handsome man who had been a World War I aviator, played at about the same skill level as Mrs. P and the two of them would sometimes play golf together in the middle of the week. That is, they did until one day when Mr. P showed up at the course shaking with anger. He walked out to where they were playing and a heated discussion ensued. Mr. and Mrs. P walked back to the parking lot together and we never saw them again.

MS had what seemed to me the best job in the world. He was a traveling salesman for the golf department of Wanamaker's department store in Philadelphia, then the country's premier outlet for British golf clubs, golf balls, clothing and Church and McAfee golf shoes. I knew that if I ever found myself there with money to spend I would be in golf heaven.

Each summer he would come to Indianapolis and hire me to guide him to the area golf courses where he would make sales calls. I truly enjoyed it. The tedium of being in an automobile all day was relieved because I got to sit in on his calls and become current on the world of golf equipment.

Joseph H. Cowan

TC was a literate bantamweight boxer. To be his caddie was to be educated about the books of the day, especially the works of Studs Terkel who was just beginning to make his mark, and to hear how TC's handlers were stealing him blind. A prominent contender, he nearly became champion several times. After my relocation to California I did not hear about him again.

HS, an aspiring singer, had a 1931 Cord sedan that was truly a masterpiece of style and power. Once I asked how fast it would go. He said he didn't know, that the one time when he was ready to go flat-out he reached 110 mph and then saw a farmer's truck coming onto the highway about a mile away. Out of caution he slowed down and never chose to test the speed again.

When he decided to go to Hollywood to try out for the movies he sold the Cord to get money for the trip. The second-hand car that he bought broke down on the way and just getting there took all of his money. I had developed a pretty good rapport with him and we wrote letters back and forth until about 1939 or 1940 when I was able to use my railroad pass to travel to Southern California. While in Hollywood and I went to the only address I knew. He was long gone. No one knew where.

AH, a handsome unmarried woman who traveled for a living and played excellent golf would come alone to Willowbrook when she was in Indianapolis and pick up a game. It was enjoyable to be her caddie because of her easygoing Southern demeanor and skillful play. She attracted some attention because she had what was considered a job that only a man could handle.

Miss X was a beautiful young woman whose name I never learned. She would come by herself to the golf course in a 16-cylinder Cadillac convertible sedan, engage me as her caddie and play alone. One day when she was about to tee off, Bob H. came along and said that he would like to join her. I thought he was brash to do so but when she asked me if that was customary, I said that it was not unusual. So they had a sociable round. She never returned.

RH was an elected law enforcement official who liked to play golf with three friends at the break of dawn. He would arrange for caddies to show up about 4:30 A.M. The way they played golf made it clear that they had been partying all night. After a while they quit coming and we wondered why. Later we learned that they all were in jail, convicted of bribery.

LL, a retired railroad agent, was so thin he seemed but a skeleton draped with dry skin. The Burlington railroad had just introduced a diesel-electric streamlined passenger train on a mid-west run and LL's favorite theme was saying what folly it was because steam locomotives would never be replaced. We caddies knew better because John Wayne, just getting his start, had made a B movie about that train and it operated successfully.

There was an especially interesting telephone conversation that I overheard. A very successful automobile dealer was obsessed with golf but married to a woman who had a low opinion of it. One Sunday morning he played really well. He was eager to play again in the afternoon and phoned his wife to obtain clearance. I heard him say, "Honey, if you will let me play golf this afternoon I'll buy you that new Lincoln."

Mr._____ was handsome, educated, socially well connected, a good golfer, better looking than any professional actor. And he was totally worthless. When he became too old to be supported openly by his father he tried to sell cars, but was a failure because he acted as though his sales prospects were beneath him.

Gossip had it that he had impregnated a young woman from the country club set. In those days pregnancy outside of marriage was an absolute no-no, especially among the upper crust. The young caddies used to snicker and say that the first baby could come at any time and that all the others took nine months.

Her family sent her away to await birth and he picked up stakes and went to Hollywood. I never saw him in a moving picture nor did I ever see his name among the screen credits. It couldn't have happened to a more deserving person.

Quite an education for one not yet eighteen. Perhaps I should have paid them.

WHEN THEY PLAYED

Throughout the 1930s the standard workweek was five and one-half days. The weekend began shortly after noon on Saturdays when the parking lot began to fill. Golfers were on the first tee just as soon as shoes could be changed. Sunday was about as active as it is today. Only after World War II did the five-day workweek, long advocated by William Randolph Hearst, become standard. Once looked upon as a dangerous radical because of views like this, at the time of his death he was thought to be a rabid right-winger, yet his support for the five-day workweek never wavered.

HOW THEY ARRIVED: THE DEL MONTE SPECIAL

The Southern Pacific's Railroad's Del Monte Special operated between Monterey and San Francisco on a schedule that served both the affluent Monterey Peninsula residents going to San Francisco for the day to see either their trust officers or their lawyers and return in time for dinner, and golfers either going to or coming from the Pebble Beach, Cypress Point or Monterey Peninsula Club golf courses. Its parlor car was something of a junior grade Orient Express; rich passengers and a steward who knew all the regulars and prepared drinks and sandwiches according to their individual tastes. It stopped at the Del Monte Station, about one mile from the end of the line where golfers staying at the Del Monte Hotel were met and driven there.

The hotel's rates included meals, either on its grounds or at the Lodge at Pebble Beach that was an appendage of the hotel. It also provided transportation to and from the golf courses.

Early in World War II the Navy took over the hotel as a school for officers of high rank and the Lodge at Pebble Beach became the principal element of the operation. Change is a certainty but not always for the better.

A personal note: in early September of 1942 I had a glorious weekend both on the parlor car and at the hotel. Upon my return to San Francisco I took the Soldier's Oath and, as the Army did with all other conscripts, I was given time to settle my affairs. Then I was back on the Del Monte Special; this time in coach. Destination: an eight man pyramidal tent at the U. S. Army Reception Center, Presidio of Monterey.

(*Presidio* relates to when California was a colony. Under Spanish law colonial settlements consisted of three parts; the civil (alcalde), the religious (mission) and the military (presidio). The Presidios of Santa Barbara, Monterey and San Francisco lived on through Spanish, Mexican and United States rule).

STORIES THE PARKING LOTS TOLD

Many of the cars then in the parking lots of golf courses would not be recognized today. Gone forever are the Nash, Rockne, Hudson, White, Essex, Elcar, Jewett, Moon, Auburn, Stutz, Marmon, LaSalle, Hupmobile, Reo, Willys-Knight, the air-cooled Franklin and more. On the other hand Chrysler Company automobiles, newly introduced in 1924, were present wherever there were a large number of automobiles. The aristocrats of the parking lots were the 12-cylinder Packards and the 16-cylinder Cadillacs.

Many cars had options to accommodate golf clubs. Touring cars had upright stands on their running boards, as did some coupes and convertibles. Others had small doors on the sides of the trunks through which golf clubs could be inserted and removed side ways.

The height of show-off chic was a young man smoking a pipe, driving a convertible with golf clubs mounted on the running board, and a German Shepherd at his side.

While growing up in Indianapolis, I saw many electric cars at school as mothers came to deliver or pick up their children and many a department store electric delivery truck, but I never saw an electric passenger vehicle in a golf course parking lot. Their 30-mile range was too short and, besides, they were bought only the very staid. These cars were electric-period. Hybrid automobiles were far away, though a few hybrid railroad locomotives were then coming into use.

HOW PLAYERS DRESSED

Over-the-calf stockings, either plaid or plain, were worn by those who wore knickers, and ankle or crew socks were worn by those who wore slacks. A player wearing knickers would sometimes also wear lightweight, white ankle socks over regular stockings that made him look something like a racehorse whose ankles had been wrapped.

Wool was the material of choice for good stockings even though they had a short life. The seemingly useless ankle socks by reducing friction between sock and shoe kept the fragile wool socks from popping out at the heel and toe. Wearing ankle socks over wool socks became obsolete in the forties when life-extending blends were introduced.

Though it now seems old-fashioned, socks of the day, either wool or cotton, had to be held up with garters because there were no elastic tops. Also wool socks had to be hand washed and then dried on a sock frame so they would not shrink to infant size.

About 1934 the Gaucho shirt (said to be inspired by Argentine cowboys) became popular with golfers for winter use. It replaced the patterned lumberjack shirt and was a wool or wool-type single color, long-sleeved shirt with four or five hemispherical covered buttons with loop fasteners. We see this type of shirt today except that button and loop have been replaced by trouser-type flys.

Before 1930 Knicker suits were popular. The jackets and knickers were of matching fabric, and the jackets had patch pockets and belted backs. Though I had heard George Stark, former pro at the Inwood Country Club on Long Island, talk about how many he once owned, I did not see one until 1937. It was worn by a gentleman on a streetcar going to the Claremont Country Club to join the gallery at the Oakland Open. Matching Argyle stockings and sweater rounded out his outfit. I was on the same streetcar on the way to seek a caddie job. I never thought that he was on a streetcar because he could not afford an automobile, just assumed that he was there because it was the most efficient way to get to the country club. Even today in downtown San Francisco many members of the Bohemian, Pacific Union, Olympic, Family and University Clubs use public transit to get to and from lunch at their respective clubs.

Though Horton Smith, Craig Wood and Gene Sarazen continued to wear knickers in the thirties, slacks became the trousers of choice as the decade rolled on.

Although golf shoes have not changed much in appearance, waterproofing them was something that came along much later.

Synthetic fabrics were in the future, but the wool and cotton sweaters worn then could be worn today and not look out of place—unless, of course, they were washed carelessly.

The connection between exposure to the sun and skin cancer had not been made and it was generally fashionable to have a deep tan; for many, unfortunately, it still is seen as a badge of health and vigor.

Many golfers played bareheaded, not knowing what they risked. Eighteen-year-old Andy was a caddie who never wore headgear. Though he came from a fair-skinned family, his face had tanned to a deep mahogany and the sun had bleached streaks of platinum in his dark hair. You could see that lesions were starting to develop on his skin. In 1937 I moved to California with my family and I never saw or heard about him again.

Those who did not play bareheaded wore caps or hats with never a logo to be seen. Logo mania was in the distant future and baseball caps came to golf only after early World War II newsreels showed them being worn by senior naval officers.

WHAT THEY DRANK

When the decade began Prohibition was still in effect and consumption of alcohol was illegal. Some country clubs forbade it on their premises because it was against the law. Others closed their eyes to what went on.

Legal drinks included Near Beer, lawful so long as its alcohol content did not exceed a very low threshold. It looked like beer but was said not to taste very good. I never knew because at age 11 or 12 I was not qualified as a critic.

Many people had an aversion to carbonation and favored Birely's fruit flavored, fizzless drinks. Coca Cola was as much in favor then as it is now, and some breweries produced full lines of soft drinks that sold well. However the repeal of Prohibition sent them back to their original businesses.

7-Up came to market about 1932 and sold well from the start. As a caddie-snack bar attendant I was the one who had to answer questions.

Joseph H. Cowan

When customers asked what it was, I looked at the label and answered, "It's lithiated lemon soda, sir." That seemed to satisfy, although I doubt that either of us knew what it meant. I still don't.

I must mention summer candy—something we may never see again. In those times chocolate melted immediately in hot weather and created a gooey mess. Some stores froze them as way of unloading their surplus. I never understood why people would buy brick-hard candy, but they did. Candy makers adapted to hot weather by coating their bars with a white glaze that did not melt, sometimes adding a sprinkling of coconut or shredded nuts. Finally the chemists developed a chocolate coating that could stand the heat and that was the end of "summer candy."

ABOUT THE PROS

HOW PROS WERE PAID. In many if not most cases a pro's income derived solely from the proceeds of merchandise sales, club care and lessons. Those who received salaries were few and far between. It was regarded as disloyal for members to buy their equipment anywhere but the pro shop. The feeling was so entrenched that it led to a touring pro being barred from PGA-sponsored events because he endorsed Walgreen's Peau-Deux line of golf clubs and golf balls. Today this would have put him out of business, but back then the only meaningful events from which he was barred were the State and National PGA Championships.

BECOMING A PRO. One way to become a pro was by saying so. If you said that you were a pro and had the game to go with it there was no one to say that you were not. The PGA, founded in 1916, was struggling for recognition, and then did not have the strength to enforce entry requirements

Joseph H. Cowan

There were three kinds of pros, Gypsy Pros (my own term), Club pros and Playing Pros. A sub-classification within the Club Pros was the Contract Pro.

Gypsy Pros. Gypsy Pros were those who became so by declaration, but were without club affiliation. They lived by their golfing skills, now and then winning prize money in tournaments, but more often winning it from their playing partners. Sometimes they lost and could not pay. I recall a cashless loser saying, "I'm sorry but I didn't bring any money."

The same man drove some distance to compete in a tournament that had an attractive purse. He failed to win anything and, in a chain of events too long for discussion here, lost ownership of his car. Afterwards he said to a competitor from his hometown, "I'm going to hop a freight home; will you please take my clubs in your car?" But he was resourceful. He landed on his feet and was one of those who made the cut at the 1935 U. S. Open at Oakmont in Western Pennsylvania.

Club Pros. .The prevailing way to become a Club Pro was to be a well-dressed caddie, articulate enough to relate easily to the members. After that it was Learn-by-Doing and advancement was up to the individual. Some advanced to good Head Pro jobs; others remained perpetual Assistants. (As this was Depression time, Club Pros who were cast adrift when their clubs went out of existence became unwilling Gypsy Pros).

Education was hardly ever a consideration in hiring. Craig Wood and Sam Parks, Jr. were among the very few college-educated pros.

Playing Pros. Playing Pros were those who had established strong name recognition. In those days news reports of tournament results included a player's name, club affiliation and location.

For example:

55th Open Championship
Held at the Colonial Club, Fort Worth, Texas, June 5-7, 1941
Yardage-7005 Par-70
1,048 Entries; 163 Starters
57 Contestants who completed 72 holes

Place		Score	Prize
1	Craig Wood, Winged Foot CC, New York	284	$1,000
2	Denny Shute, Chicago. Ill.	287	$800
3	Johnny Bulla, Chicago, Ill	289	$650
	Ben Hogan, Hershey CC, Pa.	289	$650
5	Herman Barron	291	$216.67
	Paul Runyan, Metropolis CC, New York	291	$216.67
7	E. J. (Dutch) Harrison, Chicago, Ill	294	$150
	Harold (Jug) McSpaden, Winchester CC, Mich	294	$150
	Gene Sarazen, Lakeview CC, New York	294	$150
10	Ed Dudley, Broadmoor CC, Colo.	295	$125
	Lloyd Mangrum, Monterey Park, Calif.	295	$125
	Dick Metz, Oak Park, Ill	295	$125
13	Henry Ransom, Glen Garden G&CC, Texas	296	$100
	Horton Smith, Pinehurst GC, NC	296	$100
	Sam Snead, Hot Springs, Va	296	$100
	*Harry Todd, Lakewood CC, Texas	296	medal
17	Lawson Little, Monterey Peninsula, Calif,	297	$50
	Byron Nelson, Inverness CC, Ohio	297	$50
19	Vic Ghezzi, Deal GC, New Jersey	298	$50
20	Gene Kunes, Holmesbury CC, Pa	299	$50
21	Ralph Guldahl, Chicago, Ill.	300	$50
	Clayton Heafner, Linville G&CC	300	$50
	Johnny Palmer, Badin, NC	300	$50
24	Jimmy Hines, Lakeville CC, New York	301	$50
25	Joseph Zarhardt, Jefferson CC, Pa.	302	$50
26	Sam Byrd, Merion Cricket Club, Pa.	303	$50
	Herman Keiser, Firestone CC, Ohio	303	$50
	Johnny Morris, Tuscaloosa CC, Ala.	303	$50

Joseph H. Cowan

	Henry G. Picard, Twin Hills G&CC, Okla.	303	$50
30	Jim Ferrier, Elmhurst CC, Ill.	304	$50
	Jerry Gianferante, Brattleboro CC, Vermont	304	$50
	*Marvin H. (Bud) Ward, Spokane, Wash.	304	medal

*Amateur

Many clubs, seeing an advantage to having their names linked with winners, contracted with successful players to represent them. Nearly all tour players had club affiliations though few spent a lot of time at the club they represented.

Contract Pros. Contract Pros (again my term) were pros 1) who consistently finished in the top brackets on the Tour, and were sought after for endorsements or 2) who had attained enough regional success to induce the manufacturers to tie them up in case they gained endorsement value. The beginning annual retainer was $1,500.

THE CELEBRITIES, TITANS, AND STARS

Viola Dana, Richard Arlen and Tony Martin were generally present at Northern California tour events.

VIOLA DANA, a silent movie star, was married to long-hitting Jimmy Thompson and accompanied him on the tour.

RICHARD ARLEN, a prominent movie star, would bring his family; they represented the ideal image of an American family: handsome father, beautiful mother (Jobyna Raulston from Tennessee's Sequatchie Valley), and well-scrubbed children. His golf was good but not distinguished; it was their presence that made heads turn.

Motoring from Southern California to the San Francisco Bay Area even in his Model J Dusenberg Touring Car (canvas top, no windows) could not have been a total picnic. Driving along the coastal route meant climbing out of the Los Angeles basin over the Conejo Pass, along the chilly, fog-bound ocean-side road via Santa Barbara, Santa Maria and Pismo Beach, and climbing the mountain from sea level up to San Luis Obispo. Next, depending on the time of year, you had to get through either the very hot or very cool Salinas Valley into San Francisco. In short, the Arlens traveled though several climate changes in an open car to get from there to here.

But driving via the San Joaquin Valley was no better. Coming over the Grapevine Pass could also be either too hot or too cold. Once over the pass the route was flat as a pool table, sometimes steeped in convection fog, and also nearly always too hot or too cold.

TONY MARTIN, also likely to be present, played at the skill level of Richard Arlen. Again, people liked to see him and his custom car: a Packard chassis and a body designed by a Los Angeles coach maker who made rakish convertibles for the movie crowd. Known as Al Morris in his pre-Hollywood days, he had attended St. Mary's College in nearby Moraga and was especially popular in the San Francisco Bay Area. I last saw him when he was a spectator at the Oakland Open in early 1942 and later read that he became an Army Air Force sergeant, flying the Burma Hump every day.

BING CROSBY AND BOB HOPE played in and sponsored events in Southern California but seldom came north. Crosby's clambake was held at Rancho Santa Fe until sometime in the 1950s when it was relocated to the Monterey Peninsula after he had moved his family to Burlingame, south of San Francisco.

THE TITANS

Because of the long shadows they cast in the twenties, Chick Evans, Walter Hagen, Bobby Jones, Maureen Orcutt, Virginia Van Wie and Glenna Collette Vare cannot be left out of any discussion of golf in the 1930s

CHICK EVANS

(1890-1979)

Although he was the outstanding golfer of his time, he made a contribution to the quality of life that will live on long after his golfing record. An ex-caddie who did not have the means to attend college, he established the Evans Caddie Scholarship Program.

His tournament record:

1907-   Chicago Amateur Champion

1908-   Chicago Amateur Winner

1909-   Western Amateur Winner

1910-   Winner, Western Open

1911-   North and South Amateur Winner; French Amateur Winner

1911-   Chicago Amateur Champion

1912   Runner Up, U. S. Amateur; Western Amateur Winner

1914-   Runner Up, U.S. Open; Western Amateur Winner

1915-   Western Amateur Winner

1916-   Winner-U. S. Open and U. S. Amateur

1920-   U. S. Open, tied for 3rd place; Western Amateur Winner

1921-   Western Amateur Winner; Walker Cup Team

1922-   Runner Up, U.S. Amateur; Western Amateur Winner; Walker Cup Team

1923-   Western Amateur Winner; Walker Cup Team

1924-   Walker Cup Team

1927-   Runner Up, U. S. Amateur

1928-   Walker Cup Team

Joseph H. Cowan

    1944-   Chicago Amateur Winner

When Evans was on his winning streak the rules provided that an amateur golfer could accept prize money and retain his amateur status if the money were placed in trust.

Evans had no interest in turning pro so he established the Chick Evans Caddie Scholarships program, and the Western Golf Association assumed its administration in 1930. In 2004 more than 500 member clubs, 34,000 WGA Par Club members and 100,000 WGA Bag Tag Program members support the Evans Scholars Foundation, the nation's largest individually funded scholarship program.

Although the Schoolboy Caddie is all but extinct where I play, he (and she) seem alive and well in Western Golf Association territory. Mr. Gary Holaway of the WGA staff told me that the 2004 applicants for Evans Scholarships outnumber openings by about five to two (say 500 applicants seeking 200 slots).

WALTER HAGEN

(1892-1969)

He was born in near Rochester, New York and he died in Traverse City, Michigan. But what a roller coaster in between. His record of major tournaments won made him one of golf's titans and his off-the-golf-course life made him one of the Western world's best-known bon vivants. But nature finally caught up with him. After his golfing and living-it-up days were behind him, royalties from the sale of Walter Hagen golf clubs relieved him of financial stress in his final years when he was a very sick man.

His tournament record boggles the mind. In 1914 and 1919 he won the U. S. Open. In 1915, 1922,1923, 1924, 1928, and 1929 he won the British Open. In 1921, 1924, 1925, 1926 and 1927 he won the Professional Golfers Association (PGA) Championship.

You probably would not have seen him on the tour in the thirties because his serious campaigning was behind him, though he continued to compete selectively and to play very profitable Exhibition Matches all over the World. He already had been what others wanted to be—many times over.

I saw Walter Hagen but twice, once about 1932 when he and Joe Kirkwood played an Exhibition Match at Meridian Hills Country Club in Indianapolis. Seventy years later I learned that Jim McNamara, my classmate at St. Joan of Arc Grammar School and a future classmate of Walter Hagen, Jr. at Notre Dame, was there too. The second time I saw him was about 1941 in the lobby of the St. Francis Hotel in San Francisco where he was waiting for his automobile (a Robin's Egg blue Lincoln Continental) to be brought to the Carriage Entrance that major hotels had at that time. As always, his clothes were splendidly tailored and his demeanor commanding.

In those days the typical San Franciscan did not seek autographs or attempt conversations with celebrities. In today's language, it would not have been "cool." Though many in the lobby must have known who he was, he strode in without anyone openly signaling their recognition or awe. In fact, San Francisco gained a reputation for leaving celebrities alone, and many well-known people journeyed from Hollywood to San Francisco on weekends, knowing they could be out in public and left undisturbed.

People forget that Walter Hagen revolutionized the business lives of professional golfers by being something of an equal rights activist. Before his time, pros at British clubs had the status of near-servants. At tournaments they entered the clubhouse through side or back doors and hung their clothes on nails that were affixed to the walls of the dreary room(s) assigned to them.

Hagen changed all that. He campaigned for and won the right to enter front doors and use the same locker facilities as the club members. After him things were never the same in other respects, also.

Getting there is a story in itself. The folklore of 1920s golf is full of stories about the wonderful shipboard parties when Walter Hagen was on the passenger list. A far cry from the time Avery Brundage kicked Eleanor Holm off the 1936 U. S. Olympic Swimming Team because she sipped some champagne on the crossing from New York to Cherbourg.

Among the countless tales of Walter Hagen's generosity were the naysayers. One journalist, referring to the oft-repeated statement "Walter Hagen would give you the shirt off his back" retorted in print: "Why not? After all he has a trunk full of them."

BOBBY JONES

(1902-1971)

Bobby Jones was born to an affluent Georgia family and was virtually raised at Atlanta's Eastlake Country Club. He began winning regional tournaments at an early age. 1930 was his banner year when he won the Grand Slam: then the U. S. Open, the U.S. Amateur, the British Open and the British Amateur.

By that time he had won the British Open (1926 and 1927), U. S. Open in 1923 and 1929 and been its Runner-Up In 1923 and 1929 and in 1922, 1925, 1926 and 1928. Johnny Goodman put an end to the string of being either winner or runner up when in 1929 he eliminated Bobby Jones in the first round of the U. S. Amateur at Pebble Beach. Goodman went on to win the U. S. Open in 1933 (the last amateur to do so) and later won the U. S. Amateur in 1937, one of the few who won the Open before winning the Amateur. But for the very early Masters Tournaments in which he did not do well, Bobby Jones did not play competitive golf again. This was about the time he was experiencing early symptoms of the painful ailment that bit-by-bit led to his death in 1971.

A press report told of him flubbing a chip shot and of a person in the gallery saying, "Nice work, Jones." to which Jones responded, "Thank you.

Joseph H. Cowan

GENE SARAZEN

1902-1997

He was the Tiger Woods of his day, winning both the U. S. Open and the PGA in 1922 when he was age 20 and returning the next year to win the 1923 PGA. After that he won the Western Open in 1930, the British Open and the U. S. Open in 1932, the PGA in 1933 and the Masters in 1935. He was Runner Up in the 1926 Western Open, the 1940 U. S. Open for which he won $800. He had placed 10th in the 1938 U. S. Open and won $106.25

When I was age 13 anything that had happened 10 years earlier seemed right out of the Stone Age. So when I read of Gene Sarazen winning both the U. S. Open and the PGA in 1932 after doing the same thing in 1922 it seemed to he that he had risen from the tomb.

The only time he talked to me was when there was no one else in sight. It was at the 1935 Indianapolis Open near the end of a practice round day. In the near-twilight of cold October Sarazen came out of the locker room, saw me dawdling near first hole, a dog leg left (a dog leg hole is one that is crooked, going straight from the tee for up to 300 yards and then bending right or left) this one was defined by a bunker about 250 yards out. Flying a ball above and beyond the bunker would shorten the hole considerably and increase the player's chances of breaking par on the hole. He asked how the hole was played. I said that the members avoided the bunker by aiming to its right and that they did so because it was not possible to fly a ball that far. He said, "Watch this." And he hit a ball that flew far over the bunker.

MAUREEN ORCUTT

1907- ca 1982

Born in New York, her string of victories began in 1922 when she won the Metropolitan Girls Junior Tournament. She repeated in 1924. Her later major wins began in 1930 when she won the Women's Canadian Open. She also won the same event in 1931 and 1932. In 1931, 1932 and 1933 she won the Women's North and South Invitational at Pinehurst but her best play was a match she lost. In 1936, playing under her married name (Mrs. J. D. Crews), she was Runner Up in the U. S. Women's Championship, losing to the great Pam Barton of England.

VIRGINIA VAN WIE

1909 – ca 1980

Born in Chicago, Van Wie was a dominant figure in USGA women's championship tournaments between 1928 and 1934 when she retired from tournament golf. In the USGA Women's Championship she was Runner Up in 1928 and 1930. She was winner in 1932, 1933 and 1934. In those years the Runner Ups were Glenna Collette Vare, Helen Hicks and Dorothy Traung, respectively

Joseph H. Cowan

GLENNA COLLETTE VARE

1903-1987

She was the Bobby Jones of women's golf. Before her marriage in 1931 she was in the record books as Glenna Collette.

Her tournament record:

1922-   U. S. Women's Amateur Winner

1923-   Canadian Women's Amateur Winner

1923-   North and South Women's Amateur Winner

1924-   North and South Women's Amateur Winner

1925-   U. S. Women's Amateur Winner

1927-   North and South Women's Amateur Winner

1928-   Women's Western Open Winner

1929-   North and South Women's Amateur Winner

1929-   U. S. Women's Amateur Winner

1930-   Women's Western Amateur Winner

1930-   North and South Women's Amateur Winner

1930-   U. S. Women's Amateur Winner

1935-   Women's Western Open Runner Up

1935-   U. S. Women's Amateur Runner Up

STARS OF THE TIME

TOMMY ARMOUR, a native of the United Kingdom, was a casualty of World War I. One legend has it that his nickname "The Silver Scot" was derived from a silver plate that army surgeons inserted in his skull after he took a bullet in the head. Another view has it coming from his prematurely gray hair.

He migrated to the United States in the mid-twenties and then turned pro. His record in the major tournaments consisted of winning the U. S. Open in 1927, the Western Open in 1929, finishing sixth in the 1930 U. S. Open, winning the PGA in 1930 and the British Open in 1931, and being Runner Up in the 1933 Western Open.

He was renowned as a teacher and there was much locker room talk about his strength. It was said that he could move a pool cue from horizontal to vertical just by placing the small end between his fingers and rotating his wrist.

Joseph H. Cowan

PAM BARTON was a bright, shining light in the United Kingdom between 1935 and 1939. In 1935 she was Runner Up in the Women's British Amateur, in 1936 she won both the British Women's Amateur and the Women's U. S. Amateur defeating Maureen Orcutt (then Mrs. J. D. Crews) in the finals, and in 1939 she won the Women's British Amateur again. She entered the Women's Auxiliary Air Force at the beginning of World War II and continued to serve until a pilot-error airplane accident took her life early in 1943.

PATTY BERG had a stranglehold on women's amateur golf in the mid-thirties. She was Runner-Up in the 1935 U. S. Women's Amateur and its winner in 1937 and 1938. She excelled in all of the many sports in which she took part. Professional golf for women was on its way and when it arrived she won almost every event she entered.

JOHNNY BULLA is prominent in my memory though I saw him but briefly at the Indianapolis Open in 1935. I suppose it was because he was the contestant closest to me in age. I was a 16-year-old caddie and he was 21 and new to the tour. He stood about six feet four and his thick Angora sweater made him look even larger.

He finished out of the money at Indianapolis but went on to finish 63rd in the 1936 U.S. Open, 46th in a two-way tie in 1937 and sixth in 1939, Runner Up in the 1939 British Open and winner of the 1941 Los Angeles Open. During World War II he served as an airline copilot. Later he pioneered air travel for golf pros as they moved between tournament sites.

A Caddie Remembers

BILLY BURKE is in the record books as the come-from-nowhere winner of the 1931 U. S. Open when he defeated George Von Elm in a 36-hole playoff. He was also the first winner of the U. S. Open to play with steel-shaft clubs. He continued on the tour for a few years and his best showing was finishing sixth in the 1934 U. S. Open.

SAM BYRD was a major league baseball player who crossed over to professional golf and did pretty well at it. He finished 16th in the 1939 U S Open and 41st in 1940. His high spot was reaching the PGA finals in 1945, when he lost to Sam Snead.

HARRY COOPER spent most of the 1930s representing a club in Glen Oak, Illinois, but by 1939 he was playing out of the Shenecossett Country Club in Connecticut. A regular on the tour he was always a contender. In the U. S. Open he was Runner Up in 1927, placed fourth in 1930, second in 1936 ($750), third in 1938 ($650). He had won the 1934 Western Open and the 1937 Los Angeles Open.

WIFFY COX was a name unknown to me until I began working on this book, though I cannot imagine why. He consistently qualified for the U. S. Open and nearly always made the cut. For example; in 1930 he finished in an eight-way tie for 35th, in 1931 in a three-way tie for 4th, in 1932 for 5th ($500), in 1936 in a three-way tie for 5th and in 1937 in a two-way tie for 46th.

JIMMY DEMARET, a lighthearted soul, was a favorite of the writers. Though he did not finish in the top ten in the U. S. Opens of the thirties, he had a very impressive win record, including the 1935 and 1938 San

Joseph H. Cowan

Francisco Opens, the 1939 Los Angeles Open and the Masters in 1940. He would go on to win the Masters again in 1947 and 1950. In the 1937 U. S. Open he finished in a three-way tie for 16th, winning $87.50.

ED DUDLEY won both the Los Angeles and the Western Opens in 1931, was a member of the 1937 Ryder Cup Team, finished third in the Masters of the same year and tenth in the 1940 U S Open. He later served eight years as president of the PGA

OLIN DUTRA had a hot streak in the first half of the decade. In 1932 he won the PGA, the Western Open and the Metropolitan Open. He repeated the Metropolitan Open victory in 1933 and in 1934 he won the U S Open.

AL ESPINOSA, a native of Monterey, California, won the Indianapolis Open in 1935. Earlier he had been Runner Up in both the 1929 U. S. Open and the 1930 Western Open. He was a member of the Ryder Cup team in 1929 and 1931.

CHARLIE FERRERA won the USGA's Public Links Championship in 1931 and 1933. He was a San Francisco ironworker who played at the city's fog -bound Lincoln Park Municipal Golf Course that overlooks the Golden Gate Bridge. Unique about Charlie were his hands: they were so big that the grips on his clubs were built up to near the diameter of a baseball bat.

JOHNNY GOODMAN came from Omaha and his accomplishments are varied and hard to express chronologically. He eliminated Bobby Jones in the first round of the 1929 U. S. Amateur at Pebble Beach. In 1932 he was low amateur in the U. S. Open and then he won it in 1933 (the last amateur to do so). From there it was on to the Walker Cup team in 1934, 1936 and 1938. He later won the U. S. Amateur in 1937. Three others had won the Open before they won the Amateur. They were Francis Ouimet in 1914, Chick Evans in 1916 and Bobby Jones in 1924.

RALPH GULDAHL streaked across golf's horizon like a rocket. In 1930 his game was in the doldrums and by 1942 his golden touch had deserted him. But it was spectacular while it lasted. In 1933 he was Runner Up in the U S Open and its winner in 1937 and 1938. Also, he won the Western Open in 1936, 1937 and 1938—plus the Masters in 1938 and 1939. His physique bore a striking similarity to that of Ray Floyd and both had similar swings.

HELEN HICKS won the U S Women's Amateur in 1931 and was its Runner Up in 1933. After that she turned pro and affiliated with the Wilson Company, endorsing a line of clubs bearing her name. The Women's Tour was far in the future so she had few chances to compete as a professional.

BEN HOGAN did not come to the West Coast much in the 1930s. He was too busy playing his way out of Texas. Although he had failed to make the cut in the 1936 U. S. Open at Baltusrol in New Jersey, he won the 1940 North and South Open, was Runner Up in the 1941 Western Open and was winner of the 1942 Los Angeles Open (now the Nissan Open) and placed fourth in the U S Open that year. He later served in the then Army

Joseph H. Cowan

Air Force as a non-flying officer and, when World War II ended, he came out to win everything in sight.

BETTY JAMESON in the 1930s had to confine herself to amateur events because the Ladies Pro Tour was years away. In 1938 she won the Women's Texas Open, the Women's U S Amateur in 1939 and 1940, and the Women's Western Open in 1942.

KY LAFOON, part Cherokee from Arkansas, had a winning streak in the mid-'30s. In the 1933 U.S. Open he finished in a three-way tie for 26th. In 1934 he won the Atlanta, Eastern, Hershey, Glens Falls and Western Opens and tied for 23rd in the U.S. Open. That was the year in which he won the Radix (now Vardon) trophy for low average score. In 1935 he was a member of the Ryder Cup team, won the Phoenix Open, and, in the U.S. Open, finished in a four-way tie for 28th. In the 1936 U.S. Open he earned a three-way tie for 5th and collected $350. In 1937 he finished in a seven-way tie for 20th and his prize was $50. In 1938 he won the Cleveland Open. The USGA score sheet for the Open of that year does not include his name. Either he failed to qualify or he qualified and missed the cut. In the 1939 U.S. Open he was in a three-way tie for 9th and won $175.

Until I dug into the records I had not realized just how good he had been and I had wondered why Spalding had marketed a line of Ky Lafoon Golf Clubs. Indeed, the No. 2 wood shown in the cover photo is one of them.

Some writers said that he was the loudest dresser on the tour, but the few times I saw him his clothes were conventional.

A Caddie Remembers

LAWSON LITTLE was the son of a Regular Army Medical Officer who grew up on Army Reservations all over the United States and China. A member of the Monterey Peninsula Country Club at the time he made his competitive mark, he won the British Amateur and the U S Amateur in 1934 and repeated the same victories in 1935. Turning pro in 1936 he won the Canadian Open that year, the Los Angeles Open and the U S Open in 1940. He was a member of the Spalding Company's group of endorsers and there was a successful line of Lawson Little golf clubs merchandised through pro shops and sporting goods stores.

SAM PARKS, JR. who, as previously mentioned, seemed to come from nowhere to win the U. S. Open in at Oakmont in 1935, didn't exactly come from nowhere. He had finished 66th in the 1932 Open which meant that he had survived regional qualifying and made the cut. In later years, probably playing under the past champion's exemption, he won $87.50 in 1937 by finishing in a three-way tie for 16th, in 1939 he won zero by finishing in a four-way tie for 38th and in 1940 also won zero by finishing in a seven-way tie for 38th. He left professional golf in 1942 and entered the steel business.

HENRY PICARD, Ryder Cup team member in 1935, 1937, and 1939 won the Metropolitan Open in 1935 and 1939, the Masters in 1938, was Runner Up in the 1942 Western Open. In one of those years he was the top money winner with total prizes of $10,500 (rounded).

JOHNNY REVOLTA did especially well in 1935. He won the Western Open, the PGA, was a Ryder Cup team member and top money

Joseph H. Cowan

winner with total prize money of $9,543. His most distinctive feature was a shock of hair that absolutely defied comb and brush.

PAUL RUNYAN like Sam Snead always wore a porkpie hat. His slight build kept him from being a long hitter but what he lacked in distance he made up with a phenomenal short game. His major wins in the 1930s were in 1934 he won both the Metropolitan Open and the PGA, in the latter he defeated Craig Wood in a play off that went to the 38th Hole. In other events he consistently finished in the Top Ten. I last saw him at a Crosby Tournament on the Monterey Peninsula during the mid-60s. Retired from comptitive golf by then, he was successfully established in the wholesale jewelry business.

DENNY SHUTE was a big winner in the 1930s; He won the 1930 Los Angeles, the British Open in 1933 in a 36-hole playoff with Craig Wood, the PGA in both 1936 and 1937 and ended the decade in the 1939 U. S. Open with 3-way tie for first place with Byron Nelson and Craig Wood. In the first 18-hole playoff round Nelson and Wood were tied and Shute was three strokes behind and thus eliminated. Placing third, his prize was $700.

JIMMY THOMPSON with an average distance of 280 yards per drive was then the longest hitter on the tour, although there were some who contended that Craig Wood could hit almost as far. A native of Scotland, he was stocky, had sandy hair, blue eyes and a ruddy if not florid complexion. He was the person Central Casting would have sent had you telephoned and asked for an actor to play the role of a British colonel. Nearly always accompanied by his wife, silent screen movie star Viola Dana, he was a perennial favorite of the gallery.

In the 1935 U. S. Open at Oakmont he was tied for the lead after 54 holes but dropped two strokes to Sam Parks, Jr. in the final round. He finished 73-73-77-78:301 while Parks finished 77-73-73-76:299. The USGA summary states: "It was a heart-breaking Championship for many; none of the 20 leaders was able to break 75 in the final round." Three years later Thompson won the 1938 Los Angeles Open. He was a consistent money winner, good enough for Spalding to market a line of clubs under his name.

DOROTHY TRAUNG played in about every golf tournament of her time and was totally dedicated to the game, so much so that in a long-ago press interview there was discussion about her failure to hit the ball as far as her competitors. She was reported to have responded, "Yes, I know, and I plan to gain twenty pounds"

One of the Traungs of the Strecher-Traung Lithograph Company she belonged to either the San Francisco-area Lake Merced Country Club or California Golf Club, though her tournament schedule must have made it impossible for her to spend much time at her home club.

Except for the majors, tournament records are scattered. So all I have about Ms. Traung are my personal recollections and that in 1934 she was runner up in the USGA Women's Amateur Championship, losing to Virginia Van Wie, and in 1936 she won the Woman's Western Amateur. I

Joseph H. Cowan

regret being so sketchy, but, trust me, no discussion of 1930s' golf would be complete without mentioning her.

CRAIG WOOD

He was the Payne Stewart of his day. Both were tall and blonde, and could have modeled for classic Greek sculpture had they not taken up golf. He lived the life of Walter Hagen without Hagen's flamboyance or notoriety. As J. Peter Martin writes in his biography of Wood:

"Craig Wood married Jacqueline Valentine, a wealthy New York socialite in 1934 just before playing in the Masters in Augusta, Georgia. They lived in the Park Lane Hotel in New York City where they kept an apartment and a garage for his sleek, two seat, canvas top 12-cylinder Packard.

"He was a dashing figure in the social life of New York City. His wardrobe consisted of the finest silk ties, cashmere coats, tailored slacks and custom leather shoes. Wood was constantly being compared to Hollywood's leading men of that era."

He played out of the Hollywood Golf and Country Club in Deal, New Jersey in the 1930s and out of the Winged Foot Club in Mamaroneck, New York after 1940.

It is intriguing to think of how great it must have been living in the Park Lane with its mid-town location within walking distance of theaters and the outstanding restaurants on Fifty-Second Street and how he got to and from work in that wonderful Packard, just a short drive south to New Jersey and an equally short drive up to Westchester County.

Once when I was in Alaska I met someone who said he was a member of the Craig Wood Golf and Country Club. This made me think that Wood had gone to Florida and bought into a golf business. Only when I resorted to resources on the Internet did I learn that the Craig Wood Golf and Country Club is a municipal golf course owned and operated by the town of North Elba, New York. Previously, the Lake Placid Golf and Country Club, it was renamed in his honor in 1948.

Craig Wood won a lot of tournaments but he was Runner Up in even more. According to biographer J. Peter Martin his many Runner Up finishes led some members of the press to refer to him as the "Number Two Wood "

MAJOR VICTORIES

1929	Hawaiian Open
1930	New Jersey State PGA
1931, 1933, 1935	Ryder Cup Team
1932 and 1933	San Francisco Open
1933	Los Angeles Open and Pasadena Open

1934   Galveston Open and the New Jersey Open

1938   New Jersey State PGA

1940   Metropolitan Open

1941   Masters and U. S. Open

1942   Canadian Open

When he won the 1941 U. S. Open at age 39 he was the oldest person to do so up to that time.

SPECTACULAR 2ND-PLACE FINISHES

The 1933 British Open: Wood was in Britain to play in Ryder Cup matches and took advantage of the opportunity to enter the British Open; the only time he ever did so. He tied with Denny Shute and lost the playoff.

The 1934 PGA: Was still a match play event and would remain so until 1958. Wood met Paul Runyan in the 36-hole finals It was a David and Goliath playoff— Wood over six feet with weight to go with it and Runyan of slight build and no taller than 5 feet seven. They were all even after the 36th hole and Runyan won on the 38th.

The 1934 Masters: He was the leader in the clubhouse and Horton Smith, still out on the course, used his extraordinary putting skill to finish one stroke ahead.

The 1935 Masters: Once again Wood was the leader in the clubhouse when Gene Sarazen got a double eagle on the 15th hole thus tying Wood and setting up a 36-hole playoff that Sarazen won. Wood received $800 plus an additional $50 for the playoff.

The 1939 U. S. Open: There was a three-way tie for first place, Wood, Byron Nelson and Denney Shute. After the first 18-hole playoff Shute was eliminated and Nelson and Wood went on to another 18 holes. Once again Wood was the victim of a miracle shot. On a 453 yard par 4 Nelson holed out a 1-iron second shot, giving him an eagle 2.

THE EQUIPMENT

GOLF BAGS.

Back then only good players were likely to have caddie-killer golf bags loaded with full sets of clubs. When someone showed up with a light canvas bag and seven clubs or less you had a pretty good idea that he or she played poorly. But you could be fooled: there were some good players who understood that they played just as well with a few clubs as with a full set. A Western Golf Association release reports that Chick Evans won the 1916 U. S. Open with a score of 286 (71.5 strokes per round average) using only seven hickory shaft clubs And this set a record that would not be bettered until 1936.

The Tufhorse was the premier golf bag of the 1930s. Made of exquisitely crafted leather, it had no stays and squeaked like a good harness when being broken in. In addition to a hood it had two exterior pockets, one for balls, tees, etc., the other for shoes and sweaters.

A Caddie Remembers

Golf bags were also made of duck and canvas. The duck of those days was a tightly woven, thick, knobby fabric that stood up to heavy use, not what is described in today's dictionaries. Bags made of it ran the gamut from caddie-killer to lightweight carry bags.

Canvas bags were principally for beginners. They had a diameter of five or six inches and were strengthened by stays. Pockets were rudimentary, often with strap and buckle closures and just large enough for a few balls and tees.

Also made of canvas, the Sunday Bag is another story. It originated in Scotland where the devout frowned on caddies working on Sundays. For those who chose golf over chapel, it meant carry your own clubs. So someone devised an ultra light canvas bag that golfers could carry with ease.

Though they were popular elsewhere, Sunday Bags never caught on in coastal Northern California where, typically, there is fog in the morning that burns off by noon. On these mornings it is often necessary for a group that just teed off to shout back to the following players and give the All Clear. So clothing was layered, something warm enough for a foggy morning, to be removed when the sun came out. Sunday Bag pockets were barely big enough for balls and tees; certainly no room for jacket or sweater.

GOLF CLUBS

In 1930 there was no limit to the number of clubs players could have in their golf bags; every player of consequence carried a left-hand club and other extras. By the end of the decade, however, a 14-club limit had been adopted.

The all-weather grip was one of the greatest improvements made in golf clubs. Before its introduction, the arrival of rain meant a generally losing battle to keep grips dry. By 1930 the manufacturers of Walter Hagen clubs had installed grips of alternating spirals of cork and leather that looked like a barber pole in shades of brown, but they never did the job. The all-weather grip that could be useful when wet came much later.

The F. W. Woolworth Company, commonly known as the Five and Dime, had branches all over the world. They carried a complete line of merchandise from sheet music to cosmetics to toy golf clubs that were made of pot metal, a wooden shaft and cheap leather-looking grips. Even if hit head on, the sponge-rubber golf balls that went with them they could not hurt anyone. But they were great for little kids who had access to a vacant lot.

(The sale of sheet music is a story in itself. Before radio, five and dime stores and some department stores had "song pluggers" whose job it was to sit at the store piano and stimulate sales by playing and singing the new songs. Some truly big names got their start this way.)

There were many golf club manufacturers back then but, like automobile companies, few survived. Sears once sold its own line under the Aristo name and Walgreen's sold its line under Peau-Deux.

Other names that disappeared were Vulcan, Shaler, Croydon, First Flight, Wright and Ditson, A. J. Reach, and Troxel. Shaler was a maker of automobile valves and Troxel made farm implements. Wright and Ditson and A. J. Reach were later folded into the Spalding operation.

The names of Walter Hagen and Tommy Armour lived on long after both died in the late 1960s. As recently as May 2003 Tommy Armour clubs were advertised in the *San Francisco Chronicle*.

The Hagen irons had compact heads, so much so that many said there just was not enough golf club, and I agreed. But the Hagen woods were a joy to see and use. They were of pleasing design and a code on the sole plate told golfers all they needed to know. A "105" said that it was best suited to those who needed a lightweight club, "205" was for those who needed a medium weight and a "305" was for sluggers.

Joseph H. Cowan

I don't know as much about the Armour clubs as I do about the Hagen clubs, but I do recall that the Armour woods appealed to heavy hitters and its irons were a cut above the Hagen irons but not quite up to Spalding's Bobby Jones irons.

An unlikely source of decent irons was Kay Jewelers. They were steel-shaft knock offs of leading Scottish clubs. I owned a set when I entered the Army but do not remember what happened to them.

For a brief period in the mid-30s "Whippy Shafts" were in use by a few players. They were to golf what fiberglass poles were to pole vaulting. A waggle of the wrists that would normally move a clubhead about six inches would move it twelve inches or more with a whippy shaft. The player with enough discipline to slow down and synchronize his wrist movement with the speed of the club head would be rewarded with extra distance, but too few managed it.

CLUBS BY PGA

By 1930 the Professional Golfers Association, recognizing that hickory shafts were on their way out, tried to save club maker jobs by selling parts (steel shafts, club head, grips, etc,) for assembly and sale. The line was limited to irons because assembling woods was too complex to be done in a pro shop. For whatever reason the PGA line did not survive.

BEGINNER SETS

A full set of clubs was thought unnecessary for a beginner. For that reason, stores like Walgreen's and Sears offered sets with four or five clubs and a rudimentary bag for less than ten dollars.

The four-club sets consisted of a wood, a mashie (No. 5), a niblick (No. 9) and a putter. The five-club sets had these plus a mid-iron (No. 2). If bought at a pro shop, beginner sets would include a better bag and perhaps two more clubs.

THE SHAFTS

Soon after steel shafts were introduced in the 1920s the United States Golf Association (USGA) arranged for tests comparing the distance a ball would go when struck with a wood shaft club as against one struck with a steel shaft club. The findings showed that neither had a measurable advantage over the other.

From the outset True Temper was the steel shaft of choice. Strange it should have worked out that way because the True Temper Company up to then was a maker of agricultural implements, such as shovels, hoes and rakes.

Though I had heard of shafts made of ash, I never saw a wooden shaft made of anything but hickory. Each time I hear the word "hickory" I think of my Grandfather Trent who grew up in East Tennessee immediately following the Civil War and was full of the sayings of that place and time.

Joseph H. Cowan

One was, "A woman, a dog and a hickory tree, the rougher ya treat em, the better they be." Another, "It ain't what ya want that makes you happy, it's what ya git." Yet another, "Even a blind pig finds an acorn now and then."

By 1930 hickory-shaft woods were truly obsolete. I never saw one in play, though plenty were visible in rummage barrels and second-hand shops. If you were in earshot when one was swung, you would know it: its swoosh sounded like an eagle flying overhead.

THE WOODS

Yes, woods were made of wood back then. Kiln-dried persimmon, the hardest of all, was used for high quality club heads. The manufacturing process was so complex that, whatever the type of wood, it was never attempted outside the factory

HEAD COVERS

Head covers for woods were introduced about 1932. They were contoured to the shape of the club, had zipper closures and the club names (Driver, Brassie, Spoon and Cleek) were embossed in gold, or at least in gold color. Though it meant an additional task for player or caddie— each had to be removed, replaced and zipped up after the ball was struck— they were better than no covers at all. Some years later knit covers came along. They were an improvement because they were flexible and eliminated the zipping.

THE IRONS

Outlawed long before 1930 was the Backspin Club, a short-distance iron that had very deep horizontal scoring. A ball hit to the green with one of them would stop on a dime.

Another oddity was the adjustable club. Using a wing nut on a semi-circular track the player could set it to any loft he or she desired. Those who used them were considered outside the mainstream.

In the 1910s and 1920s many irons had fancy flanges, but by 1930 the leading brands had none. After Bobby Jones won the Grand Slam he affiliated with the A. G. Spalding Company and, in addition to other high-level duties, he designed clubs. The top-of-the line Bobby Jones clubs sold for about ten dollars each and the lesser line Kro-Flights sold for about five dollars.

Although the Jones clubs turned back the clock they were an immediate hit. They were flanged just like the British-produced Sunningdale irons of the 1920s Shafts were of steel and hickory, the hickory for those who did not believe that steel was here to stay.

Many of today's clubs have family trees dating back to the 1930s, perhaps earlier:

- The shallow-faced Orlimar Woods are very much like Wilson's Gene Sarazen line produced after he won both the PGA and the U.S. Open in 1932 and the Masters in 1935.

Joseph H. Cowan

- The tracks on the soles of Taylor Made woods are descended from Wilson's Turf Rider woods dating from 1935. In both cases the tracks are said to keep the club from becoming entangled in long grass.

- During its introductory period Taylor Made featured a Bubble Shaft that resembled the shafts used on Power-Bilt clubs brought out by Hillerich and Bradsby, makers of the Louisville Slugger baseball bats. Power-Bilt advertising asserted that its shafts combined the feel of hickory with the sturdiness of steel. (I had always thought that H&B entered the golf club manufacturing business when it introduced its Power-Bilt line in 1934 or 1935. Only recently did I learn that it had been making golf clubs since the mid-20s.)

- Willie Ogg irons, also by Wilson, produced no direct offspring but they did influence future design. They first appeared in the mid-30s and their outstanding feature was that each club was weighted in the toe) to ease the impact of accidentally striking the ball there.

- First Flight clubs, manufactured in Chattanooga, ranked among the best, but sales never reached the critical mass needed for effective marketing. Chandler Harper of Virginia, later to become PGA champion, was under contract to play and publicize them, but they faded away without ever achieving the niche they deserved. (The reason I remember First Flight clubs so well is that they nearly killed me. While walking along Broad Street in Chattanooga I heard a crash of glass just one step behind me. A large plate glass window had fallen from the First Flight second-floor factory and would have landed on my head had I been one pace slower)

GOLF BALLS

When the 1930s began the rules of both the British and American rule makers established 1.33 inches (centimeters?) as the diameter of golf balls. Then the USGA increased the American ball diameter. to 1.68. Many decried the loss of distance caused by the greater mass, while others said that the holes should be made larger to accommodate the bigger ball but the USGA stood fast. Some years later the British went to the American ball.

At the beginning pf the decade there were two types of ball covers, the mesh and the dimple. The mesh was a pattern of rectangles, the dimple, a pattern of semi-spherical indentations, won the contest and it is the one we use today,.

The manufacturers back then gave different names to balls with differing performance levels. You could get a pretty good idea of players' skill levels by observing the type of balls they used. Top of the line golf balls had thin covers to enhance distance. And it was not unusual for a player to begin a round with brand new high-grade ball, and on the first hole hit it imperfectly and slash it beyond playability. The manufacturers dealt with this by including in their product lines golf balls with different names and with covers of varying toughness.

Joseph H. Cowan

Two examples: The Wilson Staff ball was made for skilled players had the thin cover; and the Wilson 444 the tough cover. At Spalding the Dot, and later the Tournament, was the ball for skilled players and the Kro-Flight the tough cover. In between Staff and 444 and the Tournament there were other brand names for various levels of play. Some said that striking a bottom of the market ball was like striking a bar of soap. No wonder, they retailed for twenty-five cents.

Like automobiles, many of the brands are extinct. Names we will not see again are U.S. Royal, North British, AJ Reach, Wright and Ditson, Peau-Deux, Troxel, Goldsmith. and many others whose names elude me.

WHEN CLUBS WERE NAMED

In the beginning clubs had names but no numbers. By 1930, however, numbering was on its way and many manufacturers inscribed both name and number on each club.

The irons went like this;

Driving Iron	1	Mashie	5
Mid-Iron	2	Spade Mashie	6
Mid-Mashie	3	Mashie Niblick	7
Mashie-Iron	4	Niblick	9

It is not a mistake that number 8 is missing. I never knew why it was so late to be used, but about 1934 Croydon filled in the blank with a club angled between a Mashie-Niblick and a Niblick, gave it a number 8 and called it a Pitcher.

THE WOODS

The woods were:

Driver-1   Spoon-3

Brassie-2   Cleek-4

The word "Cleek" applied mostly to woods though some special-purpose irons bore the same name. The wood had greater loft and a more shallow face than a Spoon and was used in the rough and in tight fairway lies.

THE PUTTERS

A Putter is the club golfers use when the ball is on the green (putting surface) and they just want to roll the ball toward the hole. They come in all shapes and sizes and their usefulness is a matter of opinion. One person's jewel is another person's junk.

There were many putters, both blade and mallet. The terms relate to shape: a Blade putter is just that, a tooled piece of metal sticking out from the neck of the club head; a Mallet Putter can be any shape, though mostly it is semi-cylindrical.

Joseph H. Cowan

To me the least useful was the Spalding Cash-In. It was a thin bar of metal with rounded edges and a neck rising out of the club head at an angle. I never understood why but those who used them swore by them. (I once had one, presumably handed down from Tom Watson.) I used it disastrously for several rounds and finally decided that enough was enough. After the 18th hole at the Olympic Club Lake Course I told my playing companions that I was disabling the putter by execution rather than out of anger. I bent the shaft so the club could never be used again, placed it in a wastebasket in the locker room and went off to change shoes. When I returned the putter had been taken.

The most graceful blade was the one included in the George Nicoll set (British)—a simple blade with a slight gooseneck.

The Schenectady was a distinctive mallet putter. It had an aluminum head about the size of a Milky Way candy bar with a neck rising out of the center. Most of the ones I saw came from the shop of Otto Hackbarth, a Cincinnati pro.

Spalding's Kro-Flight putter was a simple blade with a long neck and about a one-inch gooseneck, probably the inspiration for Bobby Jones' Calamity Jane.

The very best mallet putter was the Huntley, an English import. Shaped like a half moon it had wonderful balance. If I were to see one today I would buy it.

Along the same line was the Pederson putter, like a Huntley but with a pronounced gooseneck. There was also a Pederson chipper, same as the putter but with a lofted head.

The Beckley Ralston name is one I have seen only on putters, chippers and wedges. Perhaps he was the golfing version of a Betty Crocker cake mix. A Beckley Ralston putter and chipper could have been made from a single piece of metal about five inches long and four inches deep. Think of the corners as A, B, C and D clockwise from the upper-right-hand corner. Slice it at a 45-degree angle from corner A to corner C. When corners A and B are perpendicular to the ground you have the putter and the other part becomes the chipper.

The Ralston wedge was a compact-head version of other wedges on the market.

THE GOLF COURSES

Complaints about maintenance have plagued municipal golf courses from Day One. In cities where civil service had not taken hold maintenance crews were swept out after each election. As a result employees whose principal qualification was membership in the victorious political party maintained the courses.

In cities where civil service had been introduced, the crews discovering how hard it was to get fired, became sloppy and the golf courses they were supposed to care for became just as dilapidated as those maintained by political appointees.

Major exceptions were San Francisco's Harding Park, Sharp Park and Lincoln Park municipal golf courses that in the thirties were the equivalent of most country clubs, largely because of a Board of Supervisors that demanded excellence.

A Caddie Remembers

Those who worked on the courses were called Greenskeepers in some places and Gardeners in others. Where they were called greenskeepers the boss was the Head Greenskeeper; and where they were called Gardeners the boss was the Superintendent.

The United Kingdom courses were not manicured American style and Denny Shute's statement of how he won the British Open in 1933 by beating Craig Wood in a playoff is enlightening. A nephew asked, "Uncle Denny how did you do it? The reply, 'I just went over there and played muni golf. Their championship courses are almost as shaggy as our municipal courses".

I heard of but never saw golf courses with sand greens, though I saw a photograph of a sand green at Pinehurst and know that they were installed during the early days of golf in Saudi Arabia.

Farm tractors were used to pull gang mowers (Six or eight cutting units hooked up to a single source of power) to cut fairways and rough, and manual push mowers were used to cut greens. Except for Evinrude outboards, small gasoline engines were not then reliable enough for steady use and workers walked from hole to hole dragging their equipment. Course maintenance required a larger crew than now.

Farm tractors became obsolete when the Ford Motor Car Company introduced its light weight Fordson tractor series in 1931. When intended for use on golf courses it was modified: the front end of a passenger car with no body and only a rudimentary seat and the back end of a tractor. Compared to farm tractors, they were light and fast. Let your imagination run wild and see them as Centaurs, the creatures of mythology with the torso of a human connected to the body of a horse.

Although greens needed regular watering, fairways were not always watered. In regions where summer rainfall was the norm, Nature did a pretty good job of keeping them green.

Greens were often afflicted with a turf disease called Brown Patch. The name says it all. Grass would die selectively and brown spots would appear. There was little effective treatment for this curse although the United States Golf Association (USGA), working with university agronomists, eventually brought it under control.

Ammonium sulfate was something of a cure-all, used the way aspirin is used today. When something went wrong with a green ammonium sulfate was applied first. And, if the condition did not clear up, something else was tried.

Clubs had practice fairways rather than driving ranges. Players brought their own practice balls and engaged a caddie to shag (go after and bring back) them for between 25 and 50 cents per hour. When the player had struck all his/her practice golf balls, the caddie would take them back to the player who would either continue practicing or pay the caddie and call it quits.

DRIVING RANGES

In the early 1930s, long before mechanized ball-pickup devices had been invented, stand-alone driving ranges came into being. The only way to get the golf balls back to the range shack was to have someone in the landing area pick them up while the players were banging away. A stick with an open-end tin can nailed to its end was the full extent of mechanization.

Oddly enough, golf balls seldom struck the ball pickers. Much of this was sheer chance, but it didn't hurt that the pickers hardly ever ventured closer to the practice tee than the 150-yard marker. Ankle bites caused by rolling golf balls did not count as hits.

When the practice tees were in full use we pickers were sure that golf balls would collide in mid-air; and, indeed, this did happen. But it happened when only two people were practicing.

Joseph H. Cowan

From a young boy's point of view the best thing about this line of work was that it was always available. Fill a bucket, take it to the range office and collect five cents. Fill ten buckets and collect fifty cents. Then take a bus downtown, see a movie, and later buy a milkshake.

TEE BOXES

On old courses you might see a tee box at each teeing ground. They were about two-thirds the size of an army footlocker, topless, about 30 inches high and divided into two compartments, one containing a bucket of sand, the other a bucket of water. Players made their own tees by picking up sand, dipping it in water and molding the wet sand into a mound on which to place the ball.

TEES

Manufactured tees had been patented in 1899 but were slow to catch on. As late as the 1910s tee makers were paying star players to use them. But by 1930 wooden tees, and very few celluloid tees, were universally used. There was (1) the fluted tee we use today, (2) the Reddi-Tee, a fluted tee to which had been added a flange to keep the ball from getting too close to the ground; it was still in use in 1930 but faded away because it was one-size-fits-all and (3) the celluloid tee with its cream-colored stem and red platform that was an artistic success but of little practical use—its two pieces made it too frail to withstand whacking.

WALKERS ONLY.

There were no golf carts. Whether medal or match play, tournaments went 36 holes on the final day and sometimes on the semi-final day as well. And no matter how well you played, you would never be a champion if your feet would not hold up. (in 1964, during the final round of the Amateur Public Links Tournament, William McDonald used the lunch break to go to a hospital to be treated for blistered feet. He won the match 5 and 3.) Generally, if your feet gave out or your endurance flagged, your golfing days were over.

John D. Rockefeller was the only person I know of who defeated this rule of Nature. He played from a custom motorized vehicle and, as he owned the course and everything else in sight, there was no one to stop him.

In the mid-30s some salespeople went to a golf course in Indianapolis to demonstrate a strange device called a Pull Cart. The staff decided that

Joseph H. Cowan

the cart had no future. After all, everyone knew that golf was a game of walk and carry.

In the Middle West one caddie per player was the norm. A foursome with four caddies was the size of an infantry squad. Only when caddies were scarce did they serve two players. On the West Coast caddying double was routine.

SLOW PLAY

The pace of play was much faster than today. At the very hilly Oak Knoll course in Oakland, California several foursomes would play 18 holes on Sunday mornings, eat lunch and play an additional 18 holes in the afternoon, walking all the way.

Keep in mind that on a busy day a golf course is like a one-lane road running from A to B with no turnouts or passing lanes and with 36 or more vehicles moving along it at all times. Everyone is held up if there is one slowpoke group or one group that is always looking for golf balls.

Many slow players do not know that they are slow. They just live their lives that way. At the Citizens Federal Bank in San Francisco George Clark was Personnel Manager and he never made a hiring decision until he watched an applicant walk from his office to the elevator. Applicants who walked briskly received good marks; applicants who dawdled raised questions in Clark's mind.

Joseph H. Cowan

Golfers who know they are slow and feel embarrassed about it often exacerbate the situation by inviting the group behind to go through (pass). The result of this gracious act is that the slow ones hold up another group. My friend Frank Brush of the Olympic Club contends that letting people go through only complicates the problem, that the only effective way to manage the flow is to keep up with the group ahead. Signs on both Oakmont Golf Club courses in Santa Rosa, California say it best:

"Your place on the golf course is immediately behind the group ahead of you, not immediately in front of the group behind you."

Today's TV shows on golf encourage players who cannot hit the side of a barn to dither over each shot. An example of the folly of such dithering is demonstrated by a 1933 incident in Indianapolis when the then new holes on the Willowbrook course were ready but flagstaffs had not arrived. The owner and three friends played the flagless course, not knowing the locations of the holes, and one of them (Bill Wilkerson) had a round so good that it stood as the course record for two years.

Many rounds are delayed by endlessly looking for stray golf balls. A better way was imposed by William F. Reed, Sr., a no nonsense Indianapolis 1930s golfer, who insisted that caddies and players form a skirmish line and scan thoroughly the area where the ball was thought to be. This produced no miracles but it was better than each person looking independently.

In addition to being good Mr. Reed was also canny. Well known for his putting skill, he would deliberately putt short when it made competitive sense to do so. His opponents, concluding that the green must be slow, often would compensate by putting beyond the hole.

THE STYMIE RULE
(Why Scorecards Always Had One Six-Inch Dimension)

A Stymie is an instance of a ball lying on a direct line between the hole and the ball of an opponent about to putt. The Stymie Rule, in effect in some form since the 1700s, provided that a ball could be marked and lifted only if it were within six inches of an opponent's ball. This led to all scorecards having at least one six-inch side, and most have it today.

I never saw the rule invoked and, but for the help of Ms. Patty Moran, Research Assistant at the USGA Library, I would have written with a straight face that the rule had been rescinded long before 1930. And I would have been both right and wrong. For stroke play it had been rescinded in 1891 and for match play it remained in force until 1952. My blind spot was that I had never been exposed to high-level match play.

A Caddie Remembers

Two skills were made obsolete by the rescissions, laying a Stymie and playing a Stymie. The former was striking a ball with the hope that it would block another ball's passage to the hole. It was like drawing to an inside straight but seldom as successful. The latter was using a lofted club to jump over the ball blocking passage and end up in or near the hole.

THE UNIFYING ODOR

In those days all golf shops, wherever located, reeked of shellac. Before 1930 most irons were rust-prone (Macgregor had introduced its Radite line in 1923 but they went nowhere because of poor design) Clubs stored in the pro shop were put on the buffing wheel after each use. A buffed Scottish iron would gleam like household silver, but not for long. While clubs were being cleaned and buffed they were inspected—the woods for loose wrappings and loose sole plates, the hickory shaft irons for dryness, shrinkage and breakage.

Some players had their hickory shafts rubbed with nitric acid before shellac was applied. It gave the shafts a nice mellow color but I never saw it improve anyone's game.

Until the total obsolescence of hickory, golf shops employed club makers. And in areas where winter weather shut down courses, they were the only ones with golf-related year-round employment; making custom irons in drafty, shuttered pro shops to supplement the shop's machine-made lines. (I never saw a club maker who could make hickory shaft woods). To make irons that would sell for about ten dollars each, they bought club heads in bulk (nearly all Scottish imports) for about a dollar each, hickory shafts from Kentucky for 15 cents each, grip leather and listing (a gauze-like fabric that cost about ten cents per club and was affixed to the top of the shaft between the hickory and leather).

The club maker would rummage through the barrel of club heads and choose driving-irons through niblicks (No. 1 through No. 9) that seemed most alike. They were called a "Matched Set." The term lived on long after it lost relevance, just as children who never have and never will see a steam shovel will observe a power shovel and say, "Look at the steam shovel."

Although making clubs required lots of shellac, it was club care that really ate it up. Shafts that had dried out were sanded and moisture-proofed with shellac; broken shafts were removed and replaced and, again, coated with shellac, and shafts that had become loose in the hosel (the connector between clubhead and shaft) were simply soaked overnight, allowed to dry-and— you guessed it— coated with shellac. And it was like this all over the golfing world.

RAIN AND LIGHTNING.

Many courses had shelter houses, structures with roofs but no walls, where one could find protection from rain. I do not see them now but I may be looking in the wrong places.

Though getting wet never hurt anyone, lightning kills. I lost two friends that way in 1935. One was a caddie and the other the pro at Willowbrook in Indianapolis. The sky was darkening and Max Schulz, the pro, said, "I hope it doesn't rain because these pants just came from the cleaner." Then he handed a club to Chet Burns the caddie and, as he did, lightning struck Max and passed through the steel shaft to Chet. Both died instantly. Others in the group were unharmed.

This tragic incident demonstrates how quickly bad news travels. At the time, I was spending the summer about 750 miles from Indianapolis in Lake Providence, a small Louisiana town on the Mississippi River close to the Arkansas border. The town had no newspaper of its own; one published in Monroe, some 75 miles away served it and I learned about it from that paper.

TOURNAMENTS

WHAT'S IN A NAME?

What are now the U. S. Open and the U. S. Amateur began their lives in 1895 as the National Open and the National Amateur and retained these names until the rise of golf interest outside North America and Britain made clarification necessary. Similarly, the event now known as the Nissan Open began as the Los Angeles Open in 1926. There are many such cases.

WEEKLY PRO-AMS

Pro–Am tournaments, held weekly at different courses within a reasonable drive from Indianapolis, were social as well as golfing events. Spectators would dress up and come out to observe the play.

Two-man teams, a professional and an amateur, competed at scratch (no handicaps). Prizes did not amount to much because entry fees were their only source. The winning pros received cash and the winning amateurs received merchandise orders. The sum of the cash prizes and the merchandise orders could not exceed the amount taken in from the entrants, in other words-a zero sum game.

(To digress, the origin of the phrase, "gave him the works," came from the amateur/professional milieu of track and field where it was customary for promoters to award a fine watch to the amateur winner. Often a hundred dollar bill was folded into the watch. But when the money was not there the disappointed victor would complain :"They gave me the works.")

Often caddies would go from their home courses to the Pro-Am course to carry for one of their regulars. It was said to be hazardous duty because the caddies at the course where the Pro-Am was being held had a reputation for protecting their income stream by assaulting visiting caddies. Though no one ever assaulted me, I never went to a strange course without thinking: This might be the day.

The one time I got my comeuppance was in Chattanooga where I was spending a high school semester with an aunt. I wanted to caddy at the local public course but was driven away. The black caddies who controlled the turf allowed no white caddies.

The temptation to party after the pro-am sometimes lured those whose family ties were shaky. Some players would hang around the bar and drink and sing long after they should have gone home. Caddies who had been brought to the tournament venue by them had to worry about getting home if their driver got carried away.

Joseph H. Cowan

THE INDIANA STATE JUNIOR TOURNAMENT

In practice this tournament was an unspoken two-tier event, one for those whose parents paid the expenses of their children, the other for caddies who had no family support. Entry was unrestricted and the fee was low. A caddie who wanted to compete and was disciplined enough too save for it could do so. Hitchhiking then was not considered dangerous, so travel expenses ranged from zero to minimal. Further, a hotel room cost about one dollar a night and the YMCA would put you up for fifty cents. The best meal I ever had up to that time was a 40-cent steak dinner in Anderson, Indiana during the 1934 State Junior.

THE INDIANAPOLIS DISTRICT TOURNAMENT

Early summer brought the annual tournament of the Indianapolis District Golf Association. All amateurs were welcome. As I look back from my caddie perspective I appreciate the generosity of the clubs that made their courses available. Medal Play was conducted over three days, each at a separate country club. The entry fee was modest and participation provided an opportunity to play the best local courses at bargain prices.

THE AMATEUR PUBLIC LINKS (APL)

Local public links governing bodies select the players who will represent them in the annual Amateur Public Links tournament; and after that the players compete as individuals.

In the 1930s Team Hawaii made the biggest splash. They had traveled the greatest distance, wore Aloha shirts and hatbands made from the feathers of tropical birds, startling to those of us who lived in mid-America.

The Hawaiian players I remember best were Kammy Lau and Alex Muragin I saw them when I was a caddie in the 1935 tournament in Indianapolis, and when I was a spectator in San Francisco in 1937 when I attached myself to them, and, as I might have said decades later, we "hung out" together.

The interest of Indianapolis golfers in the 1935 tournament was heightened because local player Dave Mitchell was the defending champion. The tournament was dominated by the Strafaci brothers from the New York City area, however, and won by Frank Strafaci.

We caddies were surprised when a member of the San Jose, California team liked Indianapolis so much that he stayed on and became a well-known member of the local golfing scene.

Joseph H. Cowan

LURING THE BIG NAMES

Appearance money was paid to those who were able to attract paying spectators. I believe that this is what brought Sam Parks, Jr. to the Oakland Open at Claremont Country Club in 1937.

In 1935 he had won the U. S. Open at Oakmont in Pennsylvania during a period of punishing heat and concrete-like greens. To those who asked who Sam Parks was, the answer was that, no matter how unknown, his score of 299 for four rounds was the best of the lot. He was amiable, approachable and willingly chatted with the members of the gallery who came to say hello.

SAM SNEAD'S FIRST VICTORY

The Oakland tournament in '37 was the scene of Sam Snead's first tour win. As a caddie I had little chance to wander and so saw Snead only as he hit his tee shot on the 10th hole during the final round. His swing was the second best I saw in that event. The best was that of Joe Ferrando, a San Francisco caddie. (He was also the best dressed-player in the field.)

GENERIC OPEN TOURNAMENTS

Before corporate interests hijacked golf tournaments, sponsors generally were civic groups who sought to put their localities in a favorable light and resorts that saw publicity from golf tournaments as a business development tool. If income from admission fees plus entry fees was less than the tournament expenses, they guaranteed payment of the shortfall.

As it is now, these events ran from Thursday through Sunday but then the real competition did not begin until Friday. Eighteen holes were played on both Friday and Saturday and 36 holes were played on Sunday. Thursdays were set aside for play by Pro-Am teams, consisting of one pro and three amateurs and the entry fees paid by the amateurs defrayed the sponsors' costs. A friend and neighbor in Redwood City, who should have known better, once took advantage of unrestricted entry and signed up for the San Francisco Open. He was paired with a pro and two amateurs, all total strangers. The neighbor hit his first drive, the pro rolled his eyes and it was downhill from there.

Think of the tour at that time as a streetcar line going around the perimeter of a city. Get on at a stop of your choice, pay your fare (entry fee) and play until the next stop. Then decide to get off or to pay to play further. The season was a seamless affair. If you continued to play you would eventually return to where you began.

The schedule included such spring events as the North and South Open at Pinehurst (scene of Ben Hogan's first victory in 1940) and the Invitational at Greenbrier. The summer was relatively quiet because the club pros had to look after their home bases. The autumn season kicked off at the Glens Falls (NY) Open and moved about the Northeast until Indian summer was over. Then it was off to Florida and the resort-sponsored events where the resorts jumped on newsreel coverage of golf tournaments as opportunities to showcase their weather and facilities.

Getting to Florida could be a high-spirited frolic. I recall a prominent second-level pro telling of a November when he and three colleagues reserved adjoining drawing rooms on a train from New York to Miami. As soon as the train left Penn Station they began to play poker. As the train rolled through the 30th Street station in Philadelphia someone suggested that the person ahead by the time they got to Chattanooga treat the group to chicken dinners, at the time more costly than steak. When the train arrived in Florida the winner in Chattanooga had fallen deeply in the hole; he was out the sum of his losses plus the cost of the dinners.

After Florida it was on to the spring events with a detour through coastal California where the weather was often cold and damp. This is as true today as it was then. The dependably warm desert was then mostly sand dunes and jack rabbit warrens.

The San Francisco Open, a match play event, was held annually in either January or February when anything can happen. About 1938 a light dusting of snow at tournament time led a reporter to write, "many have been cold and miserable in San Francisco but none has ever frozen to death." The same is true of the Monterey Peninsula courses at Cypress Point and Pebble Beach.

NO ENTRY REQUIREMENTS

The "Opens" were indeed open: if you were able to pay the entry fee you could play. This led to contestants as disparate as a rich automobile dealer and a poor caddie. Many amateurs with deep pockets would pay $500 to get in, play their first hole and wish they could pay $1,000 to get out.

Unrestricted entry gave rise to an informal category of contestants. Tournament sponsors, knowing well the value of big names playing at prime times, gave the unknowns tee times beginning at sunrise and, they became known as "Rabbits".

A purse of $5,000 was sufficient to attract the best players. For example, at the 1935 Indianapolis Open, played at Highland Country Club and won by Al Espinosa; there were contingents from Britain and Japan as well as the usual big names on the U. S. tour.

The economics of sending overseas teams to compete for a $5,000 purse are baffling. Perhaps they were in the U. S. on other business and just came to fly their flags. Among the Japanese I remember only Torchiro Toda. Torchy had an appealing manner. He knew no English but managed by mimicking what he heard. When an American golfer would look Torchy in the eye and say, "pretty rugged," Torchy would cheerfully respond, "pretty rugged".

Joseph H. Cowan

Torchy was invited to compete in the 1936 Masters but I do not know how well he played. Six years later our countries were at war and I hope that he was not among the hundreds of thousands of combatants and non-combatants that were killed or maimed

All I recall about the Brits was one who, scanning a threatening sky, said in precise, measured tones: "I hope it does not rain for I do not want to get wet."

IMPORTANT DEVELOPMENTS POST 1930

The following developments came about after the 1930s but they are a necessary part of any book about golf. They have to do with golf swings, putting strokes, business golf, country clubs, dumping the costs of professional sports on individual taxpayers, the role of TV as it both entertained and led to copy cat lengthening of the time it takes to play a round of golf (see SLOW PLAY), universities as vocational schools for golf course and pro shop management and as farm clubs for nearly all professional sports.

THE GOLF SWING

During the 1930s the accepted way to strike a golf ball was with the classic Payne Stewart-style fluid swing. But when Arnold Palmer, Lee Trevino and Chi Chi Rodriguez came along after 1950 with their atrocious swings and began winning steadily, it seemed that the era of the graceless hitter had come. Then Ernie Els and Payne Stewart appeared and, almost as if by magic, the day of the hitter ended and the old-time swings returned.

THE PUTTING STROKE

Aside from equipment changes, the greatest improvement in golf has been the putting. It used to be that on a putt of forty feet or more the goal was to avoid a three-putt green. Much of my thinking was colored by the comments to that effect in a Nancy Lopez instruction tape.

When I first heard a TV commentator say that Fred Couples had a 50-foot putt for a birdie I thought that he was being facetious. Only when I realized that he was serious did I understand how much putting had improved.

Up to the mid-1960s the favored stroke was the Bobby Jones-inspired pendulum activated by wrist movement. (Think of the putter as a pendulum suspended by the hands.) It was the stroke of choice until it was replaced after 1965 by what I think of as the Shoulder Shuffle that all but takes the wrists out of play.

CORPORATIONS SPONSOR, YOU PAY

A consequence of corporate sponsorship of golf tournaments, and all other athletic events with a corporate name attached, is that the individual taxpayer foots the bill. The corporations pay the expenses and deduct them from income as an advertising expense, thus paying no taxes on that money. The taxes they do not pay end up being paid by you.

UNIVERSITIES AS GOLF'S VOCATIONAL SCHOOLS

In the 1930s golf was among the most minor of minor sports, so it was a revelation to read in 2000 a *Wall Street Journal* article reprinted in the *San Francisco Chronicle* about how golf course and pro shop management are now a part of the vocational curricula of many schools of higher learning. They included Arizona State, Ferris State (Michigan), Penn State, Campbell U (NC), Coastal Carolina U, Mississippi State and New Mexico State

UNIVERSITIES AS FARM CLUBS FOR ALL PRO SPORTS

Universities provide the players for virtually all professional sports and it was sociologist Harry Edwards when he was teaching at San Jose State who first pointed out what a raw deal they get. Although nearly all professional athletes have spent some time in college, few graduate. One thing I discovered just by listening to them when they gave post-game interviews was that golfers were the most educated and basketball players the least.

A cruel joke has to do with the members of a fictional professional basketball team being found frozen to death one morning in the parking lot of a drive-in theater. They had gone there to see *Closed for the Winter.*

Joseph H. Cowan

TV: GOOD NEWS-BAD NEWS

The good news is that, like Argus with his many eyes, TV made medal-play golf tournaments exciting. Without it you had to be on the golf course and could see only what your eyes encompassed. If you were at one location and the action was occurring at another, too bad! But the TV camera moves you around to whatever is happening that is of interest, no matter where it occurs

The bad news is that the economics of TV ratings almost killed match play. Think what would have happened if TV ratings had been a factor in the U S Amateur at Pebble Beach in 1929 when Johnny Goodman eliminated Bobby Jones in the first round.

Other bad news is that commentators are obliged to talk all the time. Imagine how much chatter it would take during the final round of a match play tournament, only two players walking from shot to shot. It's too bad that it is a thing of the past but not as bad as it would be if we had to endure more contrived conversation or, even more likely, if the time were filled with commercials.

BUSINESS GOLF

Golf is overrated as a tool for acquiring new business. Not only do prospects know they are being hustled, they may not be comfortable spending the greater part of a day with someone they barely know. On the other hand, hosting golf for an existing customer is a perfectly proper way to say thank you for business already consummated.

Business golf was the most stressful part of my job as Chief Operating Officer of a bank, and I did so willingly only with existing clients. As to prospects, I knew that if a person would sell out for a round of golf, any competitor could outbid me.

When newly introduced people who played golf learned that I belonged to San Francisco's Olympic Club they lost little time in telling me how they would love to play the very difficult Lake Course, scene of several U.S. Opens and other major tournaments. So when bank officers junior to me told me that their success rates would improve if only I would invite

Mr. So-and-So to the club for lunch followed by golf on the Lake Course, I felt obliged to do so. Lunch was never a problem but when we finally got to the golf course it seemed that we had to look for a golf ball on every hole and, as we looked for the errant ball, I felt the scorn of groups playing behind us. Invariably, it was this way for most of the eighteen holes.

In over 30 years of business golf the guests with whom I was most comfortable were Charley Brown, a music executive from Seattle, Bill Wright, a realtor from the San Francisco Peninsula, and Alice B. Cooper, a male singer. The young people working in the Pro Shop knew very well who Cooper was but, except for a grandmother who said that she was seeking an autograph for a grandson, the members did not.

Coop came to the club in a battered taxi rather than a stretch limousine, brought two clubs— a driver and a putter, rented a set of clubs, tucked his rock-star hair into a beret and went out and played a very good round in very bad weather. I'll never forget how far he could hit a ball. For example, on the 440-yard or so 11th hole on the Lake Course, when the day was overcast and the turf soggy from rain during the preceding week, he reached the green with two strokes, using a driver and a 2-iron.

Bill and Charley just went out and played without fuss or delay. And the three of them provided what were among the most pleasant games of my life.

PROTOCOL

If a young person were to ask my advice saying that he or she had been invited to play business golf at a country club, I would say: (1) do not hold up play and (2) do not treat golf balls as though they were jewels. There are many places where one can buy decent, used, premium-name balls at low prices. If you cannot afford to lose them, don't use them.

When you cannot find a ball readily just drop another, take the penalty and move on. Your host will bless you for not sticking closely to the rules and going back to your original position to replay the shot. Further, if you strike a ball poorly endure it silently, find the ball and hit it again. Nothing is more useless than complaining about something you brought on yourself.

SUGGESTED READING

The accomplishments of Walter Hagen. Bobby Jones, Maureen Orcutt and Glenna Collette Vare in the twenties cast a long shadow. To understand what happened in the world of golf in the decades that followed them, I recommend the following:

Sir Walter and Mr. Jones, Walter Hagen, Bobby Jones, and the Rise of American Golf, Stephen R. Lowe, Sleeping Bear Press (now Clock Tower Press), 121 South Main P. O. Box 20, Chelsea, Michigan 48118

Craig Wood, Blonde Bomber, Son of Lake Placid by J. Peter Martin, Head Golf Professional, Whiteface Club, Lake Placid, New York. Not widely available, I found a copy at Books Plus in Lake Placid, New York. Phone: 518-523-2950

The Illustrated History of Women's Golf, Rhonda Glenn, Taylor Publishing Company, Dallas that serves as both a history and a splendid coffee table book. I located mine through Amazon.com

A Century of Golf, Western Golf Association, 1899-1999, Tim Cronin, Clock Tower Press, 121 South Main, P.O. Box 20, Chelsea, MI 48118

ABOUT THE AUTHOR

Chief Operating Officer of a bank before retiring in 1984; Cowan got the idea for this work while convalescing from removal of benign brain tumor. An attendant would bring other hospital staffers to his bedside (a) because he had been in World War II and (b) because he could talk about Golf as it was in the old days.

Though there is no shortage of those who can tell about World War II, few with personal knowledge of Golf in the 1930s are still alive.

Now living in the Oakmont area of Santa Rosa, California he welcomes readers' comments. (707-537-1681 or *cowlaf@aol.com*)